SHAKESPEARE

KING
HENRY V

NOTES

COLES EDITORIAL BOARD

Bound to stay open

Publisher's Note

Otabind (Ota-bind). This book has been bound using the patented Otabind process. You can open this book at any page, gently run your finger down the spine, and the pages will lie flat.

ABOUT COLES NOTES

COLES NOTES have been an indispensible aid to students on five continents since 1948.

COLES NOTES are available for a wide range of individual literary works. Clear, concise explanations and insights are provided along with interesting interpretations and evaluations.

Proper use of COLES NOTES will allow the student to pay greater attention to lectures and spend less time taking notes. This will result in a broader understanding of the work being studied and will free the student for increased participation in discussions.

COLES NOTES are an invaluable aid for review and exam preparation as well as an invitation to explore different interpretive paths.

COLES NOTES are written by experts in their fields. It should be noted that any literary judgement expressed herein is just that — the judgement of one school of thought. Interpretations that diverge from, or totally disagree with any criticism may be equally valid.

COLES NOTES are designed to supplement the text and are not intended as a substitute for reading the text itself. Use of the NOTES will serve not only to clarify the work being studied, but should enhance the reader's enjoyment of the topic.

ISBN 0-7740-3727-X

© COPYRIGHT 1995 AND PUBLISHED BY
COLES PUBLISHING COMPANY
TORONTO—CANADA
PRINTED IN CANADA

Manufactured by Webcom Limited
Cover finish: Webcom's Exclusive **Duracoat**

CONTENTS

WILLIAM SHAKESPEARE
LIFE AND WORKS
Biographical Sketch

The Early Years

Despite the scholarship it has spawned, our knowledge of Shakespeare's life is sketchy, filled with more questions than answers, even after we prune away the misinformation accumulated over the years. He was baptized on April 26, 1564, in Holy Trinity Church, Stratford-on-Avon. As it was customary to baptize children a few days after birth, we conjecture that he was born on April 23. The monument erected in Stratford states that he died on April 23, 1616.

William was the third child of John Shakespeare, who came to Stratford from Snitterfield before 1532 as a "whyttawer" (tanner) and glover, and Mary Arden, daughter of a wealthy "gentleman of worship" from Wilmecote. They married around 1557. Since John Shakespeare owned one house on Greenhill Street and two on Henley Street, we cannot be certain where William was born, though the Henley Street shrine draws many tourists each year. William's two older sisters died in infancy, but three brothers and two other sisters survived at least into childhood.

Shakespeare's father was fairly well-to-do, dealing in farm products and wool, and owning considerable property in Stratford. After holding a series of minor municipal offices, he was elected alderman in 1565, high bailiff (roughly similar to the mayor of today) in 1568 and chief alderman in 1571. There are no records of young Will Shakespeare's education (though there are many unfounded legends), but he undoubtedly attended the town school. Ben Jonson's line about Shakespeare's having "small *Latine*, and lesse *Greeke*" refers not to his education, but to his lack of indebtedness to the classical writers and dramatists.

On November 27, 1582, a licence to marry was issued to "Willelmum Shaxpere *et* Annam Whateley *de* Temple Grafton." On the next day a marriage bond for "Willm Shagspere" and "Anne Hathwey of Stratford" was signed by Fulk Sandells and John Richardson, farmers of Stratford. This bond stated that there was no "lawful let or impediment by reason of any

precontract, consanguinity, affinity, or by any other lawful means whatsoever." Thus, "William and Anne [were] to be married together with once asking of the banns of matrimony." The problem of Anne Whateley has led many researchers and some detractors to argue all kinds of improbabilities, such as the existence of two different Shakespeares and the forging of documents to conceal Shakespeare's true identity. The actual explanation seems to be simple: the clerk who made the marriage licence entry apparently copied the name "Whateley" from a preceding entry, as a glance at the full sheet suggests. (Incidentally, Nicholas Rowe in his biography of Shakespeare, published in 1709, well before the discovery of these marriage records, gave Anne's name as Hathaway.) The problems of marriage with Anne Hathaway — he was 18 and she was 26 — and of the bond have caused similar consternation. Why did these two marry when there was such a discrepancy of age? Why only one saying of the banns (rather than the usual three)? Why the emphasis on a possible legal impediment? The answer here is not simple or definite, but the birth of a daughter, Susanna, baptized at Holy Trinity on May 26, 1583, seems to explain the odd circumstances. It should be recognized, however, that an engagement to marry was considered legally binding in those days (we still have breach-of-promise suits today), and that premarital relations were not unusual or frowned upon when an engagement had taken place. The circumstances already mentioned, Shakespeare's ensuing activities and his will bequeathing to Anne "my second best bed with the furniture" have suggested to some that their marriage was not entirely happy. Their other children, the twins Hamnet and Judith, were christened on February 2, 1585.

Theatrical Life

Shakespeare's years before and immediately after the time of his marriage are not charted, but rumor has him as an apprentice to a master butcher, or as a country teacher or an actor with some provincial company. He is supposed to have run away from whatever he was doing for livelihood and to have gone to London, where he soon attached himself to some theatrical group. At this time there were only two professional houses established in the London environs, The Theatre (opened in 1576) and The Curtain (opened in 1577). His first connec-

tion with the theater was reputedly as holder of horses; that is, one of the stage crew, but a most inferior assignment. Thereafter, he became an actor (perhaps at this time he met Ben Jonson), a writer and a director. Such experience had its mark in the theatricality of his plays. We do know that he was established in London by 1592, when Robert Greene lamented in *A Groatsworth of Wit* (September, 1592) that professional actors had gained priority in the theater over university-trained writers like himself: "There is an upstart Crow, beautified with our feathers, that with his *Tygers hart wrapt in a Players hyde,* supposes he is as well able to bombast out a lanke verse as the best of you: and beeing an absolute *Iohannes fac totum* [Jack-of-all-trades], is in his owne conceit the onely Shake-scene in a countrey." An apology for Greene's ill-humored statement by Henry Chettle, the editor of the pamphlet, appeared around December 1592, in *Kind-Hart's Dream.*

Family Affairs

To return to the known details of his family life, Shakespeare's son, Hamnet, was buried at Stratford on August 11, 1596; his father was given a coat of arms on October 20, 1596; and he purchased New Place (a refurbished tourist attraction today) on May 4, 1597. The London playwright obviously had not severed connections with his birthplace, and he was reflecting his new affluence by being known as William Shakespeare of Stratford-upon-Avon, in the County of Warwick, Gentleman. His father was buried in Stratford on September 8, 1601, and his mother, on September 9, 1608. His daughter, Susanna, married Dr. John Hall on June 5, 1607, and they had a child named Elizabeth. His other daughter, Judith, married Thomas Quiney on February 10, 1616, without special licence, during Lent, and was, therefore, excommunicated. Shakespeare revised his will on March 25, 1616, and was buried on April 25, 1616 (according to the parish register).

Shakespeare's Writings

Order of Appearance

Dating of Shakespeare's early plays, while based on inconclusive evidence, has tended to hover around the early 1590s. Almost certainly, it is his chronicles of Henry the Sixth that Philip Henslowe, an important theatrical manager of the day, referred to in his diary as being performed during March-May, 1592. An allusion to these plays also occurs in Thomas Nashe's *Piers Penniless His Supplication to the Devil* (August, 1592).

The first published work to come from Shakespeare's hand was *Venus and Adonis* (1593), a long stanzaic poem, dedicated to Henry Wriothesley, Earl of Southampton. A year later, *The Rape of Lucrece* appeared, also dedicated to Southampton. Perhaps poetry was pursued during these years because the London theaters were closed as a result of a virulent siege of plague. The *Sonnets*, published in 1609, may owe something to Southampton, who had become Shakespeare's patron. Perhaps some were written as early as the first few years of the 1590s. They were mentioned (along with a number of plays) in 1598 by Francis Meres in his *Palladis Tamia*, and sonnets 138 and 144 were printed without authority by William Jaggard in *The Passionate Pilgrim* (1599).

There is a record of a performance of *A Comedy of Errors* at Gray's Inn (one of the law colleges) on December 28, 1594, and, during early 1595, Shakespeare was paid, along with the famous actors Richard Burbage and William Kempe, for performances before the queen by the Lord Chamberlain's Men, a theatrical company formed the year before. The company founded the Globe Theatre on the south side of the Thames in 1599 and became the King's Men when James ascended the throne. Records show frequent payments to the company through its general manager, John Heminge. From 1595 through 1614 there are numerous references to real estate transactions and other legal matters, to many performances and to various publications connected with Shakespeare.

Order of Publication

The first plays to be printed were *Titus Andronicus,* around February, 1594, and the garbled versions of *Henry VI,*

Parts II and III, in 1594. Thereafter, *Richard III* appeared in 1597 and 1598; *Richard II,* in 1597 and twice in 1598; *Romeo and Juliet,* in 1597 (a pirated edition) and 1599, and many others. Some of the plays appear in individual editions, with or without Shakespeare's name on the title page, but 18 are known only from their appearance in the first collected volume (the so-called First Folio) of 1623. The editors were Heminge and Henry Condell, another member of Shakespeare's company. *Pericles* was omitted from the First Folio although it had appeared in 1609, 1611 and 1619; it was added to the Third Folio in 1664.

There was reluctance to publish plays at this time for various reasons: many plays were carelessly written for fast production; collaboration was frequent; plays were not really considered *reading* matter; they were sometimes circulated in manuscript; and the theatrical company, not the author, owned the rights. Those plays given individual publication appeared in a quarto, so named from the size of the page. A single sheet of paper was folded twice to make four leaves (thus *quarto*) or eight pages; these four leaves constitute one signature (one section of a bound book).

Authorized publication occurred when a company disbanded, when money was needed but rights were to be retained, when a play failed or ran into licensing difficulties (thus, hopefully, the printed work would justify the play against the criticism), or when a play had been pirated. Authorized editions are called good quartos. Piratical publication might occur when the manuscript of a play had circulated privately, when a member of a company desired money for himself, or when a stenographer or memorizer took the play down in the theater (such a version was recognizable by inclusion of stage directions derived from an eyewitness, by garbled sections, etc.). Pirated editions are called bad quartos. There are at least five bad quartos of Shakespeare's plays.

Authenticity of Works

Usually, 37 plays are printed in modern collections of Shakespeare's works, but some recent scholars have urged the addition of two more: *Edward III* and *Two Noble Kinsmen.* A case has also been advanced, unconvincingly, for a fragment of the play on Sir Thomas More. At times, six of the generally

accepted plays have been questioned: *Henry VI,* Parts I, II and III, *Timon of Athens, Pericles* and *Henry VIII.* The first four are usually accepted today (one hopes all question concerning *Timon* has finally ended), but if Shakespeare did not write these plays in their entirety, he certainly wrote parts of them. Of course, collaboration in those days was commonplace. Aside from the two long narrative poems already mentioned and the sonnets (nos. 1-152, but not nos. 153-154), Shakespeare's poetic output is uncertain. *The Passionate Pilgrim* (1599) contains only five authenticated poems (two sonnets and three verses from *Love's Labour's Lost*), and *The Phoenix and the Turtle* (1601) may be his, but the authenticity of *A Lover's Complaint* (appended to the sonnets) is highly questionable.

Who Was Shakespeare?

At this point, we might mention a problem that has plagued Shakespeare study for over a century: who was Shakespeare? Those who would like to make the author of the plays someone else — Francis Bacon or the Earl of Oxford or even Christopher Marlowe (dead long before most of the plays were written) — have used the lack of information of Shakespeare's early years and the confusion in the evidence we have been examining to advance their candidate. But the major arguments against Shakespeare show the source of these speculators' disbelief to be in class snobbery and perhaps in a perverse adherence to minority opinion. The most common argument is that no one of Shakespeare's background, lack of education and lack of aristocratic experience could know all that the author knew. But study will reveal that such information was readily available in various popular sources, that some of it lies in the literary sources used for the play and that Shakespeare was probably not totally lacking in education or in social decorum. The more significant question of style and tone is not dealt with — nor could it successfully be raised. Bacon, for example, no matter how much we admire his mind and his writings, exhibits a writing style diametrically opposite to Shakespeare's, a style most unpoetic and often flat. The student would be wise not to waste time rehashing these unfounded theories. No such question was raised in the seventeenth or eighteenth centuries, and no serious student of the plays today doubts that Shakespeare *was* Shakespeare.

Shakespeare's England

The world of Elizabethan and Jacobean England was a world of growth and change. The great increase in the middle class, and in the population as a whole, demanded a new economy and means of livelihood, a new instrument of government (one recognizing "rights" and changed class structure), a new social code and a broad base of entertainment. The invention of printing a century before had contributed to that broader base, but it was the theater that supplied the more immediate needs of the greatest numbers. The theater grew and along with it came less educated, more money-conscious writers, who gave the people what they wanted: entertainment. But Shakespeare, having passed through a brief period of amateur writing, proceeded to set down important ideas in memorable language throughout most of his career. His plays, particularly the later ones, have been analyzed by recent critics in terms of literary quality through their metaphor, verse line, relationships with psychology and myth, and elaborate structure. Yet Shakespeare was a man of the stage, and the plays were written to be performed. Only this will fully account for the humor of a deadly serious play like *Hamlet* or the spectacle of a *Coriolanus*.

Life in London

During Shakespeare's early years there, London was a walled city of about 200,000, with seven gates providing access to the city from the east, north and west. It was geographically small and crisscrossed by narrow, little streets and lanes. The various wards each had a parish church that dominated the life of the close-knit community. To the south and outside were slums and the haunts of criminal types, and farther out were the agricultural lands and huge estates. As the population increased and the central area declined, the fashionable people of the city moved toward the west, where the palace of Westminster lay. Houses were generally rented out floor by floor and sometimes room by room. Slums were common within the city, too, though close to pleasant enough streets and squares. "Merrie Olde England" was not really clean, nor were its people, for in those days there were no sewers or drains except the gutter in the middle of the street, into which garbage would be emptied to be

floated off by the rain to Fleet ditch or Moor ditch. Plague was particularly ravaging from 1592 to 1594 (when the theaters were closed to avoid contamination) and 1603. Medical knowledge, of course, was slight; ills were "cured" by amputation, leeching, bloodletting and cathartics. The city was (and still is) dominated by St. Paul's Cathedral, around which booksellers clustered on Paternoster Row.

Religious Atmosphere

Of great significance for the times was religion. Under Elizabeth, a state church had developed. It was Protestant in nature and was called Anglican (or today, Episcopalian) but it had arisen from Henry VIII's break with the pope and from a compromise with the Roman Catholics, who had gained power under Mary Tudor.

The Church of England was headed by the Archbishop of Canterbury, who was to be an increasingly important figure in the early part of the seventeenth century. There were also many schismatic groups, which generally desired further departures from Roman Catholicism. Calvinists were perhaps the most numerous and important of the Protestant groups. The Puritans, who were Calvinist, desired to "purify" the church of ritual and certain dogmas, but during the 1590s they were lampooned as extremists in dress and conduct.

Political Milieu

During Shakespeare's lifetime there were two monarchs: Elizabeth I, 1558-1603, and James I, 1603-1625. Elizabeth was the daughter of Henry VIII and Anne Boleyn, his second wife, who was executed in 1536. After Henry's death, his son by his third wife, Jane Seymour (executed in 1537), reigned as Edward VI. He was followed by Mary Tudor, daughter of Henry's first wife, Catherine of Aragon. Mary was a Roman Catholic, who tried to put down religious dissension by persecution of both Protestants and Catholics. Nor did her marriage to Philip II of Spain endear her to the people.

Elizabeth's reign was troubled by many offers of marriage, particularly from Spanish and French nobles — all Roman Catholic — and by the people's concern for an heir to the throne. English suitors generally cancelled one another out by intrigue or aggressiveness. One of the most prominent was the Earl of Essex, Robert Devereux, who fell in and out of favor.

He apparently attempted to take over the reins of control, only to be captured, imprisoned and executed in February, 1601. One claimant to the throne was Mary of Scotland, a Roman Catholic and widow of Francis II of France. She was the second cousin of Elizabeth, tracing her claim through her grandmother, who was Henry VIII's sister. Finally, settlement came with Elizabeth's acceptance of Mary's son as heir apparent, though Mary was to be captured, tried and executed for treason in 1587. Mary had abdicated the throne of Scotland in 1567 in favor of her son, James VI. His ascent to the throne of England in 1603 as James I joined the two kingdoms for the first time, although Scotland during the seventeenth century often acted independently of England.

Contemporary Events

Political and religious problems were intermingled in the celebrated Gunpowder Plot. Angry over fines that were levied upon those not attending Church of England services — primarily Roman Catholics — and offended by difficulties over papal envoys, a group of Catholics plotted to blow up Parliament, and James with it, at its first session on November 5, 1605. A cache of gunpowder was stored in the cellar, guarded by various conspirators, among them Guy Fawkes. The plot was discovered before it could be carried out and Fawkes, on duty at the time, was apprehended. The execution of the plotters and the triumph of the anti-Papists led in succeeding years to celebrations in the streets and the hanging of Fawkes in effigy.

Among the most noteworthy public events during these times were the wars with the Spanish, which included the defeat of the Spanish Armada in 1588, the battle in the Lowlands in 1590-1594, the expedition to Cadiz under Essex in 1596 and the expedition to the Azores (the Islands Expedition), also under Essex, in 1597. With trading companies especially set up for colonization and exploitation, travel excited the imagination of the people: here was a new way of life, here were new customs brought back by the sailors and merchants, here was a new dreamworld to explore.

In all, the years from around 1590 to 1601 were trying ones for English people, relieved only by the news from abroad, the new affluence and the hope for the future under James. Writers of the period frequently reflect, however, the disillusionment and sadness of those difficult times.

The Elizabethan Theater

Appearance

The Elizabethan playhouse developed from the medieval inn with its rooms grouped around a courtyard into which a stage was built. This pattern was used in The Theatre, built by James Burbage in 1576: a square frame building (later round or octagonal) with a square yard, three tiers of galleries, each jutting out over the one below, and a stage extending into the middle of the yard, where people stood or sat on improvised seats. There was no cover over the yard or stage, and lighting was therefore natural. Thus, performances were what we might consider late matinees or early evening performances.

Other theaters were constructed during the ensuing years: The Curtain in 1577, The Rose in 1587 (on Bankside), The Swan in 1595 (also Bankside) and Shakespeare's playhouse, The Globe, in 1599 (not far from The Rose). There is still some question about the exact dimensions of this house, but it seems to have been octagonal, each side measuring about 36 feet, with an over-all diameter of 84 feet. It was about 33 feet to the eaves, and the yard was 56 feet in diameter. Three sides were used for backstage and to serve the needs of the players. There was no curtain or proscenium, hence the spectators became part of the action. Obviously, the actors' asides and soliloquies were effective under these conditions.

There was no real scenery and there were only a few major props. Thus, the lines of the play had to reveal locations and movement, changes in time or place, etc. In this way, too, it was easier to establish a nonrealistic setting, for all settings were created in words. On either side of the stage were doors, within the flooring were trapdoors (for entrances of ghosts, etc.), and behind the main stage was the inner stage or recess. Here, indoor scenes (such as a court or a bedchamber) were played, and some props could be used because the inner stage was usually concealed by a curtain when not in use. It might also have served to hide someone behind the ever-present arras, like Polonius in *Hamlet*. The "chamber" was on the second level, with windows and a balcony. On the third level was another chamber, primarily for musicians.

Actors

An acting company such as the Lord Chamberlain's Men was a fellowship of ten to 15 sharers with some ten to 12 extras, three or four boys (often to play women's roles) who might become full sharers and stagehands. There were rival companies, each with its leading dramatist and leading tragic actor and clown. The Lord Admiral's Men, organized in 1594, boasted Ben Jonson and the tragedian, Edward Alleyn. Some of the rivalry of this War of the Theaters is reflected in the speeches of Hamlet, who also comments on the ascendancy and unwarranted popularity of the children's companies (like the Children of Blackfriars) in the late 1590s.

The company dramatist, of course, had to think in terms of the members of his company as he wrote his play. He had to make use of the physical features and peculiar talents of the actors, making sure, besides, that there was a role for each member. The fact that women's parts were taken by boys imposed obvious limitations on the range of action. Accordingly, we often find women characters impersonating men. For example, Robert Goffe played Portia in *The Merchant of Venice,* and Portia impersonates a male lawyer in the important trial scene. Goffe also played Juliet, Anne in *Richard III* and Oberon in *A Midsummer Night's Dream.* The influence of an actor on the playwright can be seen, on the one hand, by noting the "humor" characters portrayed so competently by Thomas Pope, who was a choleric Mercutio in *Romeo,* a melancholic Jaques in *As You Like It* and a sanguinary Falstaff in *Henry IV,* Part 1; and by comparing, on the other hand, the clown, Bottom, in *A Midsummer Night's Dream,* played in a frolicsome manner by William Kempe, with the clown, Feste, in *Twelfth Night,* sung and danced by Robert Armin. Obviously, too, if a certain kind of character was not available within the company, then that kind of character could not be written into the play. The approach was decidedly different from ours today, where the play almost always comes first and the casting of roles second. The plays were performed in a repertory system, with a different play each afternoon. The average life of a play was about ten performances.

History of the Drama

English drama goes back to native forms developed from playlets presented at church holidays. Mystery plays dealt with

biblical stories such as the Nativity or the Passion, and miracle plays usually depicted the lives of saints. The merchant and craft guilds that came to own and produce the cycles of plays were the forerunners of the theatrical companies of Shakespeare's time. The kind of production these cycles received, either as moving pageants in the streets or as staged shows in a churchyard, influenced the late sixteenth-century production of secular plays, in that there was an intimacy with the audience and there was a great reliance on words rather than setting and props. Similar involvement with the stage action is experienced by audiences of the arena theater of today.

The morality play, the next form to develop, was an allegory of the spiritual conflict between good and evil in the soul of man. The *dramatis personae* were abstract virtues and vices, with at least one man representing Mankind (or Everyman, as the most popular of these plays was titled). Some modern critics see *Othello* as a kind of morality play in which the soul of Othello is vied for by the aggressively evil Iago (as a kind of Satanic figure) and passively good Desdemona (as a personification of Christian faith in all men). The Tudor interlude — a short, witty, visual play — may have influenced the subplot of the Elizabethan play with its jesting and visual tricks. In mid-sixteenth century appeared the earliest known English comedies, Nicholas Udall's *Ralph Roister Doister* and *Gammer Gurton's Needle* (of uncertain authorship). Both show the influence of the Roman comic playwright, Plautus. Shakespeare's *Comedy of Errors,* performed in the 1590s, was an adaptation of Plautus' *Menaechmi,* both plays featuring twins and an involved story of confused identities. Senecan tragedy is a tragedy of revenge, characterized by many deaths, much bloodletting, ghosts, feigned madness and the motif of a death for a death.

Shakespeare's Artistry

Plots

Generally, a Shakespearean play has two plots: a main plot and a subplot. The subplot reflects the main plot and is often concerned with inferior characters. Two contrasting examples will suffice. In *King Lear*, Lear and his daughters furnish the characters for the main plot of filial love and ingratitude, whereas Gloucester and his sons enact the same theme in the subplot. Lear and Gloucester both learn that outward signs of love may be false. In *A Midsummer Night's Dream*, the town workmen (Quince, Bottom *et al.*) put on a tragic play in such a hilarious way that it turns the subject of the play — love so strong that the hero will kill himself if his loved one dies first — into farce, but this, in the main plot, is the "serious" plight of the four mixed-up lovers. In both examples Shakespeare has reinforced his points by subplots dealing with the same subject as the main plot.

Sources

The plots of the Elizabethan plays were usually adapted from other sources. Originality was not the sought quality; a kind of variation on a theme was. It was felt that one could better evaluate the playwright's worth by seeing what he did with a familiar tale. What he stressed, how he stressed it, how he restructured the familiar elements — these were the important matters. Shakespeare closely followed Sir Thomas North's very popular translation of Plutarch's *Life of Marcus Antonius,* for example, in writing *Antony and Cleopatra*; and he modified Robert Greene's *Pandosto* and combined it with the Pygmalion myth in *The Winter's Tale,* while drawing the character of Autolycus from certain pamphlets written by Greene. The only plays for which sources have not been clearly determined are *Love's Labour's Lost* (probably based on contemporary events) and *The Tempest* (possibly based on some shipwreck account from travellers to the New World).

Verse and Prose

There is a mixture of verse and prose in the plays, partially because plays fully in verse were out of fashion. Greater variety could thus be achieved and character or atmosphere could be

more precisely delineated. Elevated passages, philosophically significant ideas and speeches by men of high rank are in verse, but comic and light parts, speeches including dialect or broken English, and scenes that move more rapidly or simply give mundane information are in prose. The poetry is almost always blank verse (iambic pentameter lines without rhyme). Rhyme is used, however (particularly the couplet), to mark the close of scenes or an important action. Rhyme also serves as a cue for the entrance of another actor or some off-stage business, to point to a change of mood or thought, as a forceful opening after a passage of prose, to convey excitement, passion or sentimentality, and to distinguish characters.

Shakespeare's plays may be divided into three general categories, though some plays are not readily classified and further subdivisions may be suggested within a category.

The History Play

The history play, or chronicle, may tend to tragedy, like *Richard II,* or to comedy, like *Henry IV,* Part I. It is a chronicle of some royal personage, often altered for dramatic purposes, even to the point of falsification of the facts. Its popularity may have resulted from the rise of nationalism, nurtured by the successes against the Spanish, the developing trade and colonization, and England's rising prestige as a world power. The chronicle was considered a political guide, like the popular *Mirror for Magistrates,* a collection of writings showing what happens when an important leader falls through some error in his ways, his thinking or his personality. Thus, the history play counselled the right path by negative, if not positive, means. Accordingly, it is difficult to call *Richard II* a tragedy, since Richard was wrong and his wrongness harmed his people. The political philosophy of Shakespeare's day seemed to favor the view that all usurpation was bad and should be corrected, but not by further usurpation. When that original usurpation had been established, through an heir's ascension to the throne, it was to be accepted. Then any rebellion against the "true" king would be a rebellion against God.

Tragedy

Tragedy, in simple terms, meant that the protagonist died. Certain concepts drawn from Aristotle's *Poetics* require a tragic

hero of high standing, who must oppose some conflicting force, either external or internal. The tragic hero should be dominated by a *hamartia* (a so-called tragic flaw, but really an *excess* of some character trait, e.g., pride or *hubris*), and it is this *hamartia* that leads to his downfall and, because of his status, to the downfall of others. The action presented in the tragedy must be recognizable to the audience as real. Through seeing it enacted, the audience has its passion (primarily, suffering) raised, and the conclusion of the action thus brings release from that passion (*catharsis*). A more meaningful way of looking at tragedy in the Elizabethan theater, however, is to see it as that which occurs when essential good (like Hamlet) is wasted (through disaster or death) in the process of driving out evil (such as Claudius represents).

Comedy

Comedy, in simple terms, meant that the play ended happily for the protagonists. Sometimes the comedy depends on exaggerations of man's eccentricities — comedy of humors; sometimes the comedy is romantic and far-fetched. The romantic comedy was usually based on a mix-up in events or confused identity of characters, particularly by disguise. It moved toward tragedy in that an important person might die and the mix-up might never be unravelled. But, in the nick of time, something happens or someone appears (sometimes illogically or unexpectedly) and saves the day. It reflects the structure of myth by moving from happiness to despair to resurrection. *The Winter's Tale* is a perfect example of this, for the happiness of the first part is banished with Hermione's exile and Perdita's abandonment; tragedy is near when the lost baby, Perdita, cannot be found and Hermione is presumed dead. But Perdita reappears, as does Hermione, a statue that suddenly comes to life. Lost identities are established and confusions disappear, but the mythic-comic nature of the play is seen in the reuniting of the mother, Hermione, a kind of Ceres, with her daughter, Perdita, a kind of Proserpina. Spring returns, summer will bring the harvest and the winter of the tale is left behind — for a little while.

What is it, then, that makes Shakespeare's art so great? Perhaps we see in it a whole spectrum of humanity, treated impersonally, but with kindness and understanding. We seldom

meet in Shakespeare a weeping philosopher: he may criticize, but he criticizes both sides. After he has done so, he gives the impression of saying: "Well, that's the way life is; people will always be like that — don't get upset about it." This is probably the key to the duke's behavior in *Measure for Measure* — a most unbitter comedy, despite former labels. Only in *Hamlet* does Shakespeare not seem to fit this statement. It is the one play that Shakespeare, the person, enters.

KING HENRY V

Sources

Major Sources

Shakespeare's chief source for the history plays was the second edition of Raphael Holinshed's *Chronicles of England, Scotland, and Ireland* (1586). *Henry V* follows the *Chronicles* more closely than usual. Some of the scenes — the discussion of the Salic Law and Henry's claim to the French throne, the conspiracy at Southampton, the siege of Harfleur and the happenings at the French court — do little more than change Holinshed's prose into Shakespeare's verse. Naturally, the wars against France must be compressed in the drama. Almost two-thirds of Holinshed's chronicle of Henry deals with events after the Battle of Agincourt, but Shakespeare, with an apology in the prologue to Act V, leaps nimbly from the English victory at Agincourt in 1415 to the Treaty of Peace at Troyes in 1420.

The episodes with Falstaff's old companions, to whom Corporal Nym has been added, are Shakespeare's own, as is the king's night walk in disguise through his army before the battle.

Various chronicles, as well as popular story, made Henry a model of kingly virtue. Polydore Vergil, who came to England as collector of Peter's pence (an annual papal tax on householders), wrote a critical history of England in Latin (1534-55), the flow of which he interrupted for a most uncharacteristic eulogy on Henry. The main source of Holinshed's work was Edward Hall's *The Union of the Noble and Illustre Families of Lancastre and York* (written in 1548 and possibly read by Shakespeare), in which Henry is described as "a king whose life was immaculate and his living without spot . . . a shepherd whom his flock loved and lovingly obeyed. . . ." Holinshed piled on similar praises: "a king of life without spot, a prince whom all men loved . . . his virtues notable, his qualities most praiseworthy . . . a pattern in princehood, a lodestar in honor, and mirror of magnificence."

Among the virtues of this pattern in princehood that Shakespeare notes and stresses are Henry's understanding of the common man and his concern with the responsibilities rather than the privileges of his high office.

Possible Sources

Two earlier plays by unknown authors may have contributed ideas or incidents to Shakespeare's play. *The Famous Victories of Henry V,* first produced in 1594, pictures Henry's swift reformation upon assuming the crown and includes the dauphin's gift of the tennis balls and the wooing of Katherine. *The Wars of Cyrus,* printed in 1549, contains a description of Cyrus similar to the Archbishop of Canterbury's picture of Henry in Shakespeare's play. The 1594 play also has the Emperor Cyrus tour his camp, incognito, on the eve of battle, as Henry does.

Historical Background

Not in the order of writing, but in the chronological sweep of history, *Henry V* is the fourth in Shakespeare's series of eight history plays. Covering the years from spring, 1414 to spring, 1420, it deals with the mature life of Henry V of England, traditionally considered the ideal Christian king. Of his predecessors, Richard II had been weak in public virtue and his own father, Henry IV, had been weak in private virtue. Henry V, fortified by the wide experiences of his youth, surpassed his predecessors in both. He was viewed by the Elizabethans as a source of power and order in the stormy history of England during the century from the beginning of the reign of Richard II to the end of that of Richard III. Troubled years began with the deposition and death of Richard II (1399), after which war and devastation were suffered throughout the land until the overthrow of Richard III (1485) and the establishment of harmony when the houses of York and Lancaster were united in the marriage of Elizabeth of York and Henry VII, first of the Tudors. The Tudor line continued through Henry VIII to Queen Elizabeth I, who reigned when these plays were written.

Genealogical Tables

TABLE I
The English Succession

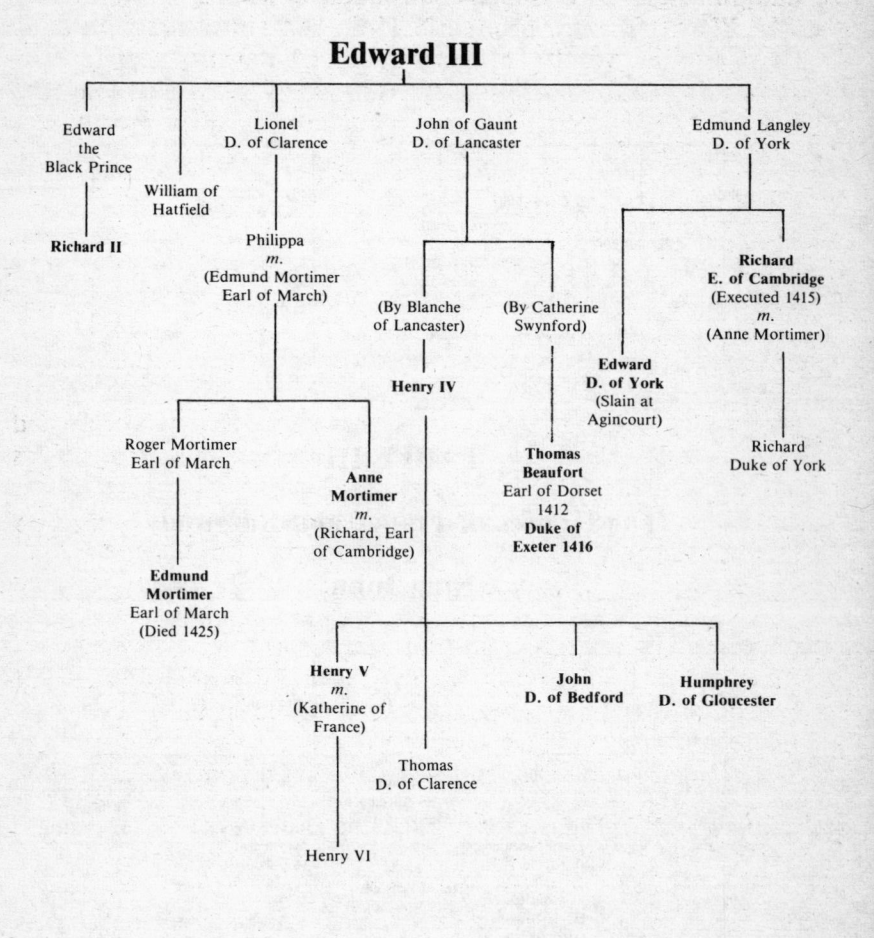

Edward III

Edward
the
Black Prince

Richard II

William of
Hatfield

Lionel
D. of Clarence

Philippa
m.
(Edmund Mortimer
Earl of March)

Roger Mortimer
Earl of March

Edmund
Mortimer
Earl of March
(Died 1425)

John of Gaunt
D. of Lancaster

(By Blanche
of Lancaster)

Henry IV

Anne
Mortimer
m.
(Richard, Earl
of Cambridge)

(By Catherine
Swynford)

Thomas
Beaufort
Earl of Dorset
1412
Duke of
Exeter 1416

Edmund Langley
D. of York

Richard
E. of Cambridge
(Executed 1415)
m.
(Anne Mortimer)

Edward
D. of York
(Slain at
Agincourt)

Richard
Duke of York

Henry V
m.
(Katherine of
France)

Thomas
D. of Clarence

Henry VI

John
D. of Bedford

Humphrey
D. of Gloucester

TABLE II

The French Succession

Philip III

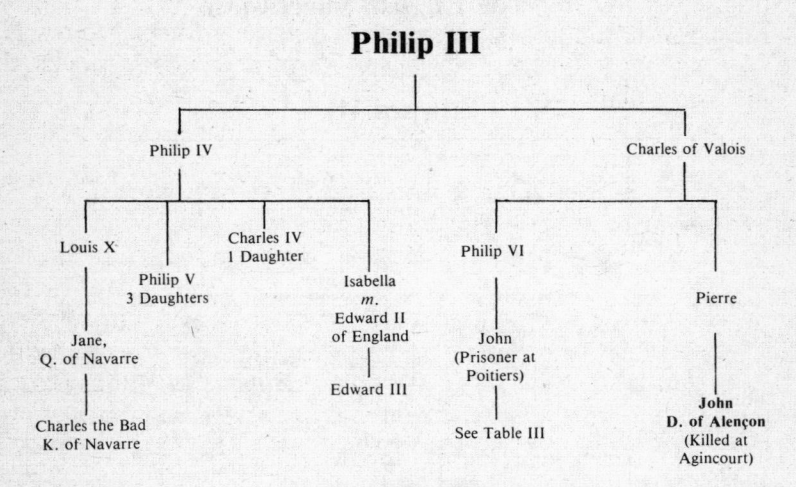

TABLE III

The Houses of France and Burgundy

King John

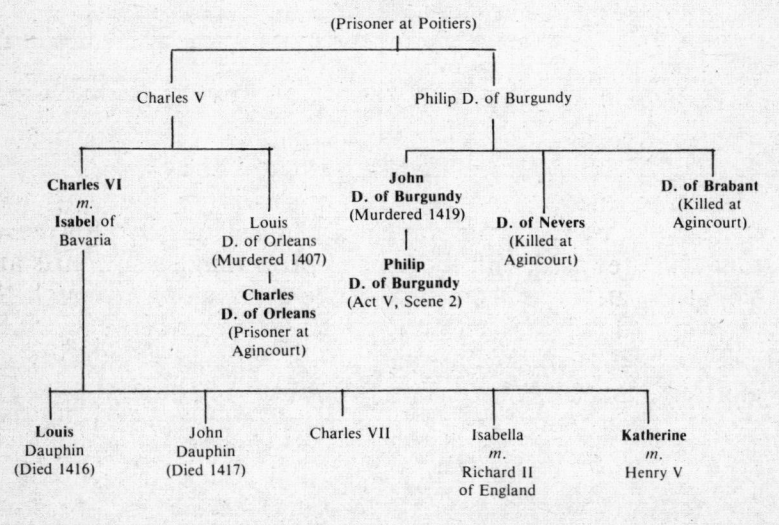

Apologetic Prologues

The prologues in this play, not printed until 1623, are unusually apologetic. Shakespeare seems sensitive to the inadequacies of the stage for the presentation of besieged cities and turbulent battlefields. Indeed, Ben Jonson's *Every Man is His Humor,* first staged in 1598 and printed in 1616, mocks the historical plays, which

> with three rusty swords,
> And help of some few foot-and-half-foot words,
> Fight over York and Lancaster's long jars,
> And in the tiring-house bring wounds to scars.

However, this prologue may not have been spoken in 1598, for Jonson's play was put on by Shakespeare's company, which performed the very sort of play Jonson was ridiculing. But the criticism of grand historical plays being performed upon a puny stage is a recurrent one. Some, indeed, state that the play is more effective when read than when acted. Yet, inevitably, in times of national urgency, when war threatens or rages in the land, the rousing rhetoric of *Henry V* echoes in English hearts. The king's prayer before Agincourt, says A. L. Rowse, "still moves one to tears," as does his inspiring praise of his countrymen, from highest rank to lowest.

In only one other play, *Pericles*, does Shakespeare give us five prologues and an epilogue. For that play, they are put in the mouth of the poet, Gower, who had told the story of the play in his *Confessio Amantis* (1390). The second edition of *Henry V* — omitting passages in praise of Richard II — is dedicated to Henry IV. Here, the prologues, spoken by the chorus, seem to come from the mouth of the author and serve three purposes: (1) they apologize for the inadequacy of the stage and for the actors who are faced with the task of presenting royal courts and embattled armies; (2) they carry the story along, through the months and (from Act IV to Act V) the years between the incidents; and (3) they contribute to the spirit of patriotism and glorification of the king. The first words of the first prologue are: "O for a Muse of fire!" — and in the play the Muse grants the poet her favor.

Plot Summary

The play opens with the Archbishop of Canterbury and the Bishop of Ely discussing the government's threat to confiscate church revenues. They hope to gain the king's favor by supporting his plans for war with France. King Henry's determination to "bend (France) to (his) awe, or break it all to pieces" is strengthened by the arrival of the French ambassadors, who present Henry with tennis balls — a contemptuous reference to his wild youth. The king replies with dignity and spirit that he will turn these tennis balls into ammunition for guns. Thus, he declares war on France and begins preparations for the invasion.

The second act of the play introduces characters familiar from *Henry IV*: Bardolph, Nym, Pistol and Mistress Quickly. Pistol announces that Falstaff has died of plague, and Mistress Quickly (now married to Pistol) provides a touching description of the fat knight's last moments. The three rogues decide to join Henry's army in Southampton.

In Southampton, Henry detects a conspiracy against his life. He orders the three traitors, Lord Scroop, Sir Thomas Grey and the Earl of Cambridge, to be executed.

The siege of Harfleur by the English is underway as the third act opens. King Henry is seen encouraging his men to assault the walls of the town. Bardolph, Nym and Pistol, in cowardly fashion, hide in the rear, but the Welsh captain, Fluellen, drives them forward. Fluellen and the Irish captain, MacMorris, then argue over the tactics of the siege. The English army overpowers Harfleur, which falls because the dauphin, failing to take the English assault seriously, has denied the town any aid. Later, Henry leads his tired and hungry army toward Calais. At Agincourt, the English army is met by the French troops, commanded by the dauphin and the constable of France.

The scenes of battle in the third act are relieved by a shift in scenery to the French king's palace, where we witness Princess Katherine receiving a lesson in English from her maid and, in another chamber, the king, his son and several nobles discussing the war and expressing their surprise at the successful advance of the English.

On the eve of the Battle of Agincourt, King Henry disguises himself as a common soldier and discusses with several of his

men the responsibilities of the king during a war. After playfully arranging a quarrel with one of the men, Williams, Henry returns to a serious state of mind. He considers the emptiness of ceremony, contrasting his own position with that of his poorest subjects, utters a brief prayer and returns to his army.

Meanwhile, in the opposing camp, the overconfident French eagerly anticipate their victory over the war-worn English. In the ensuing battle, however, the French are soundly defeated by the English. Although the French have superior equipment and larger armies, inadequate leadership accounts for their severe defeat at the hands of Henry's well-commanded army.

After the battle is over, Fluellen, wearing Henry's glove, meets Williams, who challenges him to fight. Fluellen is about to take up the quarrel when Henry and some of his lords appear. The king explains how he had earlier exchanged gloves with Williams as tokens by which they could recognize and fight each other should they both survive the battle. The events of the day are reviewed, and a thanksgiving service is ordered throughout the army.

Fluellen encounters Pistol who, on a previous occasion, had scoffed at him. The Welshman inflicts deserved punishment on the boastful bully by making him eat the distasteful leek, the Welsh national emblem.

The last scene depicts the English and French representatives meeting in council at Troyes to arrange the terms of peace. The Duke of Burgundy acts as mediator and speaks eloquently on the virtues of peace. All Henry's demands are accepted, and peace is concluded. King Henry woos Princess Katherine, whom, according to the terms of the peace, he is to marry. The French queen, Isabel, pronounces a blessing upon the royal union.

Characters in the Play

KING HENRY V: The rebellious Prince Hal of Shakespeare's *Henry IV*. Now the ruler of England, he is a brave, wise and praiseworthy monarch.

DUKE OF GLOUCESTER: Henry V's youngest brother.

DUKE OF BEDFORD: Another brother of Henry. He is honorable and courageous.

DUKE OF EXETER: Henry's uncle and chief advisor.

DUKE OF YORK: Second cousin to Henry. He is an older man and a heroic knight.

EARL OF WESTMORELAND: Another of the king's advisors.

EARL OF WARWICK; EARL OF SALISBURY; DUKE OF CLARENCE: Members of the king's royal party. They contribute nothing significant to the play.

ARCHBISHOP OF CANTERBURY: Appears only in the first scene. His chief concern is the preservation of church lands.

BISHOP OF ELY: He shares the interests of the archbishop.

LORD SCROOP: A former close and admired friend of the king, later arrested for treason.

SIR THOMAS GREY: Another of Henry's former friends who is arrested with Scroop.

EARL OF CAMBRIDGE: A third member of the treasonous group.

SIR THOMAS ERPINGHAM: A gentleman who is in command of part of Henry's army.

FLUELLEN: A Welsh captain in Henry's army. He has a quick temper.

GOWER: An English captain in Henry's army. He is quieter and less colorful than Fluellen.

MACMORRIS: An Irish captain in charge of the mines.

JAMY: A Scotsman. Also a captain in Henry's army.

JOHN BATES; ALEXANDER COURT; MICHAEL WILLIAMS: Common soldiers in Henry's army. Williams is the most developed and interesting character of the three.

24

BARDOLPH: A coward and a thief. He is known for his red nose and swollen cheeks.

PISTOL: Like Bardolph, he is a familiar figure from *Henry IV*. He is now married to Mistress Quickly.

NYM: Another low-life character. He has a melancholy temperament and tends to make pessimistic remarks.

BOY: Originally in the service of Falstaff, he later falls in with the three rogues after the fat knight dies.

MISTRESS QUICKLY: As in *Henry IV*, she is hostess of an Eastcheap tavern. In this play, we find her married to the scoundrel, Pistol.

FALSTAFF: He does not actually appear in the play, but we learn of his illness and death.

CHARLES VI: King of France. He is much older than Henry and does not take an active part in battle.

DAUPHIN (LEWIS): The childish and irresponsible heir apparent to the French throne.

CONSTABLE OF FRANCE: Commander-in-chief of the French army and an honorable patriot.

DUKE OF BURGUNDY: An independent ruler who appears only in the final scene as a mediator in the signing of the treaty.

DUKE OF ORLEANS: Cousin of the dauphin and his defender.

DUKE OF BRITAINE: A powerful lord who is eager to fight off the advancing English army.

DUKE OF BOURBON: Another member of the French court with strong anti-English sentiments.

DUKE OF BERRI: Another French noble who vigorously opposes the English.

RAMBURES; GRANDPRÉ: Less important commanders in the French army. Grandpré is killed in action.

MONTJOY: A French herald who carries messages to Henry.

ISABEL: Queen of France. She pleads for peace in the final scene of the play.

KATHERINE: Daughter of the French king and queen. She is beautiful, charming and spirited.

ALICE: The princess' maid and companion.

Summaries and Commentaries by Act and Scene

ACT I · PROLOGUE

Summary

The speaker, simply referred to as the chorus, calls for the highest kind of inspiration for the presentation of this great subject — kings, princes, kingdoms and war. He asks for lenience in the judgment on the actors, who have presumed to offer their interpretation of so mighty a theme. He says it is absurd to hope to have this round wooden theater even suggest the wide extent of France. The audience will therefore have to multiply this place a million times in their imaginations and help out the actors by supposing this little playhouse does represent two mighty monarchies. The actors are relying on the audience to see kings, armies and horses in their mind's eye so that they can supply the background for the events. The audience must also take the lapses of time for granted.

Commentary

Shakespeare prefaces each act of the play with a prologue. Employed in the tradition of the Greek drama, these chorus-prologues help to raise the stature of the play to the heroic or epic level. Immediately, "the warlike Harry" is established as an epic hero. The apology for the stage and actors serves to increase the stature of the hero and his actions. We are led to think, not of the players, but of the actual king.

Perhaps with the contrast between the "Muse of fire" and the Mars-like Harry and the actual frail humans that must appear in the drama, Shakespeare is establishing in this very first speech the all-important theme of humanity versus kingship. Was Harry really the superhuman hero that the historians had immortalized? Could a man be so dedicated to his ideal of kingship that he could rise above human frailty? How much does he have to give up along the way? What does it take to make a great king? As *Henry V* unfolds, we watch for Shakespeare's views on these questions.

The time that we are asked to span with our imagination covers six years. Henry reigned from 1413 to 1422. The events of the first act, beginning the war with France, occurred in 1414.

Acts II, III and IV present happenings of 1415. Act V jumps the intervening years to the Treaty of Troyes and the betrothal of Henry and Katherine in 1420.

Shakespeare often staged battles without apology, as in *Troilus and Cressida*, *Antony and Cleopatra*, *Coriolanus*, *Macbeth*, *Julius Caesar* and *Henry IV*. Here, he apologizes for the inadequacies of the stage in order to suggest the epic quality with which he wishes to endow this drama. His subject is not merely this war, but war in general and what it involves; not merely Henry, but kingship and what it demands. Through the heroic language and vigorous rhetoric of the prologue, Shakespeare ingeniously uses his very apology to emphasize the grandeur of his scope.

While the elevated rhetoric of *Henry V* has been generally praised as matching the military tone of the play, some have criticized this aspect of the drama. Samuel Johnson protested:

> Nothing shows more evidently the power of custom over language than that the frequent use of calling a circle an O could so much hide the meanness of the metaphor from Shakespeare that he has used it many times where he makes his most eager attempts at dignity of style.

Johnson overlooks the fact that Shakespeare is at this moment seeking to picture *in*significance. This theater — this O, this nothing — must be enlarged by the audience's imagination to the range of two kingdoms. (The great Elizabethan theaters were, of course, round buildings.)

Note the comparisons that mention animals: "leashed in like hounds," crouched at Henry's heels, the "cockpit," the pounding horses. Through the play runs an undercurrent theme of war as the clash of beasts. The poet, William Butler Yeats, said that Shakespeare watched Henry, not as a great soul, but "as one watches some handsome spirited horse."

The historian, Rowse, without other evidence than "the personal, the proprietary tone of these speeches," declares that in the Elizabethan productions of the play, the role of chorus — the speaker of the prologues and epilogue — was taken by Shakespeare himself.

ACT I · SCENE I

Summary
The Archbishop of Canterbury and the Bishop of Ely are discussing a bill pending in parliament that, if passed, would strip the church of much of its material wealth. In reply to Ely's question about what can be done to prevent this serious threat to the funds of the church, Canterbury compliments the king, and the two holy men embark on a description of Henry's sudden reformation from irresponsible prince to perfect king, praising his holiness and wisdom. Returning to the question at hand, Canterbury reveals a proposition that he has made to the king to sway him to the side of the church. Canterbury intends to convince King Henry that he has the legal right, derived from Edward III, to wear the crown of France. He will encourage Henry to go to war in a righteous quest of his lawful heritage. As an added incentive, the clergy will supply the king with a great sum of money. Although they do not say so, the churchmen hope that, in return, the king will not allow the damaging bill to pass. Canterbury states that the king seemed to sympathize with the church's position when he explained it to him but their discussion was interrupted by the French ambassadors' request for an audience with the king — which they now must attend.

Commentary
This scene presents the clergy's motive for encouraging Henry's claim to the French throne. It introduces with great immediacy the theme of war and the personal motives behind the national action. The audience is also reminded of the sudden conversion of Prince Hal when (at the close of *Henry IV*, Part II) he became King Henry V. Their comments prepare us for the entrance of the king, a wise and dedicated monarch.

With subtle artistry, Shakespeare leads us to look beneath the surface of these holy men's discussion. To Ely's question concerning the damaging bill "But what prevention?" Canterbury responds: "The king is full of grace and fair regard." This is followed at once by Ely's answering chant: "And a true lover of the holy church." On the surface, all is holy, as the devout churchmen praise their king. Through this description of the virtuous king, Shakespeare established the popular image of

28

Henry, "the mirror of all Christian kings," that his audience expected. Beneath the surface, however, there is a hint of deceit in these dealings. There is an aura of bribery, calling into question not only the moral honesty of the churchmen who would promote war to serve their own ends, but also the fabled integrity of this ideal king.

Canterbury's words describing Henry's reformation sound the opening notes of one of the more subtle themes of the play:

> Consideration like an angel came
> And whipped the offending Adam out of him,
> Leaving his body as a paradise
> T'envelop and contain celestial spirits.

Henry is indeed a man that has been "whipped." As we shall see, however, it is not an angel that has made him holy. Rather, he has himself subdued all warm humanity in order to fulfil the kingly destiny to which he is so deeply dedicated. "The offending Adam" that has gone out of him has removed, not merely man's tendency to sin, but all the vibrant and careless happiness, all the bubbling joy in human existence, that were represented by Falstaff and the other companions of Prince Hal.

These churchmen do not have to be viewed as hypocrites. Shakespeare neither praises nor criticizes; he observes and (with varying degrees of directness or subtlety) he displays. Here he lets us see that it is just those men in public life who most admire their leader that most seek to use him to forward their own concerns.

Canterbury's listing of Henry's virtues covers all the attributes of a proper ruler: Henry discusses divinity like a learned man of the church; he is a master in the affairs of the commonwealth; he is competent and inspiring in matters relating to war; and

> Turn him to any cause of policy,
> The Gordian knot of it he will unloose,
> Familiar as his garter; that when he speaks,
> The air, a chartered libertine, is still,
> And the mute wonder lurketh in men's ears
> To steal his sweet and honeyed sentences.

In civil as well as military virtues, he is a true king.

ACT I · SCENE 2

Summary

This scene opens with a meeting of the king and his lords in the royal castle. The king will not receive the French ambassadors until he has heard from the Archbishop of Canterbury his opinion and received assurances from him as to the justness of his cause, meaning his claim to the throne of France. When Canterbury and Ely are brought in, Henry requests the former very solemnly to give him his carefully considered advice as to the rightness of his claims to the throne of France. Henry is especially anxious to hear Canterbury's advice on the question of the Salic law, which the French revived to oppose his claims. Henry puts the responsibility upon Canterbury, in the sight of God and having in mind the bloodshed that may follow, to tell him truly where he stands in religion and morality. To a modern audience, it sounds somewhat as though Henry ought to take this terrible responsibility himself and not pass it on to Canterbury or anyone else. It sounds a little, too, as though he had already made up his mind and simply wants competent religious authority.

Canterbury rises to his cue and, in one of the longest and most tangled speeches in the play, tells the king to proceed against the French. In brief, he says that the Salic law never applied to France nor the throne of France, that it was a local provincial regulation (and a temporary one at that) that applied to a small district called the Salique land and that that land was never in France but is at present in Germany in a district called Meisen. There seemed in those far-off times among a savage people to be a local reason for forbidding the claiming of a ruler's position through a woman, but it never applied in France, for several of the kings of France have obtained in the past their succession to the crown through the rights of their mothers. He adds that the French are simply setting up this artificial barrier now for the purpose of preventing the king from claiming that the marriage of his ancestor, Edward II, to Queen Isabella of France still entitles Henry to the French throne.

Canterbury thus assures Henry that he may with right and conscience make this claim, and he takes the moral responsibility for this advice upon his own head. Further, he cites scriptural authority from the Book of Numbers to back up the king's claim. Then he urges Henry to go ahead and imitate the glorious

military exploits of his great-grandfather, Edward III, and of his great-uncle, the Black Prince, to bring fame and glory to England. Ely echoes this urgent advice. Exeter adds that all the ruling powers of Europe are expecting him to take this course. Westmoreland adds his words to the same effect, while Canterbury repeats his urging and pledges huge financial support from the church.

The king brings up the question of danger from Scotland while he is away. Canterbury thinks the northern defences are strong enough. The king reminds them all of the invasion from Scotland when Edward III began the Hundred Years' War in France. Canterbury dismisses the danger and, although Westmoreland and Exeter seem to think there is something in it, he makes another long and fine speech advising the king that if the kingdom is as well organized as a colony of bees, he can leave three quarters of his available forces at home and beat the French with the other quarter.

The king says he has made up his mind to invade France. He confidently calls in the French ambassadors, who are accompanied by attendants carrying a barrel full of tennis balls.

The French ambassador, reassured by Henry that he may speak freely and safely, delivers a very insulting message from the dauphin. He announces that France cannot be won by a frivolous youth, and that Henry had better forget his claims and confine himself to pleasure (hence the present of tennis balls).

The king answers with poise and dignity that he is to tell the dauphin that he will be over shortly to play such a match as all France will regret, and these tennis balls may turn to cannon balls.

The ambassadors leave under safe-conduct, and the king turns to the lords and says he hopes to make the sender blush for this insult. He gives orders then for immediate preparation for the invasion of France.

Commentary

We meet Henry in this scene and observe his strong character and his need to be assured that his cause is just. Events move rapidly toward the war that comprises the body of the play. The long speeches, in heroic diction, reinforce the sense of historic action.

In the dialogue between Henry and his counsellors can be seen the dramatization of a problem that was quite topical in Shakespeare's time. The motivations and moralities of war were very much in the minds of Elizabethans. They wrote many treatises and sermons dealing with the question of whether or not a Christian state ought to make war. The general conclusion reached was that war in defence of a worthy cause can be sanctioned, but only after all other efforts to settle the dispute have failed. Queen Elizabeth herself, like Henry, sought moral justification from the clergy, asking the approval of Archbishop Whitgift before intervening on behalf of the Netherlands against Spain in 1585. There was also an Elizabethan example to match the archbishop's offer of aid for Henry's French wars. Although the church had been going through a period of extreme difficulty, when England faced the great threat from Spain in the year of the Armada, 1588, the clergy provided the crown with large quantities of money and arms. The audience no doubt compared Henry's wars with those of its own day.

Some historians say that the war with France was in truth a righteous war. They contend that, Henry's claims being justified under feudal law, it was his duty as a virtuous king to fight for his lawful rights. The Salic Law, it is further argued, was indeed a shabby contrivance to deny the claims of Edward III. (In Shakespeare's time, English pretension to the French throne was still very much alive.) Other historians argue just as heatedly that Henry undertook the wars purely for reasons of pride and selfishness, in total disregard of the anguish and bloodshed he would cause. It seems unlikely, however, that Shakespeare meant to convey either of these extreme views. He is showing us rather, as he always does, that life is neither all black nor all white. Perhaps there was a measure of legality in Henry's claim to the French throne, but there was also a degree of shabbiness in his attempts to shirk all moral responsibility for a war that would benefit only himself. According to Holinshed, whose chronicles were the major source of the hero-king legend, Henry V, on his deathbed,

> protested unto them that neither the ambitious desire
> to enlarge his dominions, neither to purchase vaine
> renowne and worldlie fame, nor any other considera-
> tion had moved him to take the warres in hand; but
> onlie . . . prosecuting his just title . . . he was fully

persuaded by men both wise and of great holiness of life . . . without all danger of God's displeasure or perill of soule.

When Shakespeare paints his picture of the hero-king, he presents the same facts as Holinshed, but he takes a deeper, more subtle look at a hero-king who could not help but have some human blood in his veins. The king is crisp and business-like. Despite the great length and emotional intensity of the speeches of his council, Henry coolly responds as though his mind had been made up in advance and, now that the public show of convincing him is over, they can get down to the business of the details.

His demand to know whether the war with France is just, however, allows Henry to maintain his moral dignity. His earnest request that Canterbury speak only the truth serves three dramatic purposes. It presents Henry as a model of kingly virtue; it shifts the responsibility for a war of conquest to the holy church; and it reveals Henry's need to appease the tender conscience he had inherited from his father (who had every reason to be afflicted with a bad conscience for his deposition of Richard II). It also exposes the gestures of a man in public office, who first makes his decision and then secures the people's approval and God's blessing.

The Archbishop of Canterbury performs the function of a good churchman, making it possible for the king to do, with an easy conscience, that which he has already decided to do. The presence of the French ambassadors in Henry's court and the ambassadors' words to the king make it evident that Henry's ultimatum to France had been made before this turning to the archbishop for spiritual sanction. Even at the end of *Henry IV*, Part II, this war is prophesied. In that play's closing speech Lancaster says:

I will lay odds that ere this year expire,
We bear our civil swords and native fire
As far as France. I heard a bird so sing,
Whose music, to my thinking, pleased the king.

Having first determined upon his course, then having the church take the responsibility for it, Henry now seizes upon the

dauphin's scornful gesture first to boast, but then to throw the blame for the coming evils upon the French prince:

> But I will rise there with so full a glory
> That I will dazzle all the eyes of France,
> Yea, strike the Dauphin blind to look on us.
> And tell the pleasant prince this mock of his
> Hath turned his balls to gunstones, and his soul
> Shall stand sore charged for the wasteful vengeance
> That shall fly with them; for many a thousand widows
> Shall this his mock mock out of their dear husbands,
> Mock mothers from their sons, mock castles down;
> And some are yet ungotten and unborn
> That shall have cause to curse the Dauphin's scorn.

Henry's reply to the dauphin's insult begins in the language of tennis — "When we have matched our racquets to these balls" — to declare that the game will win for him the crown of France. Then he reflects:

> We understand him well,
> How he comes o'er us with our wilder days,
> Not measuring what use we made of them.

As he talks, however, his anger takes hold of him so that he loses his kingly calm and lapses from the royal "we" to the personal "I." He recaptures his poise to blame the dauphin for the slaughter that is to come and to dismiss the ambassadors "with safe conduct."

The long speech on the Salic Law comes almost phrase for phrase from Holinshed. It is interesting to note, however, that all the French rulers here mentioned to justify Henry's claim through the female line were usurpers!

Also note that Henry does not await the reply of the French, but resolves upon war before the ambassadors come in. And his tone is that of the tyrant conqueror:

> France being ours, we'll bend it to our awe
> Or break it all to pieces.

The long speech of Canterbury, comparing the various roles among the honeybees (workers, soldiers, drones,

monarch) to the well-ordered commonwealth (the kingdom magnifying the pattern of the hive) develops a figure frequent in Shakespeare's time. Sir Thomas Elyot introduced it in his study of *The Gouvernour* (1531). It occurs in Lyly's popular *Euphues*, which Shakespeare may have had in mind, for the end of the speech of Canterbury piles on similes in the affected manner of the "euphuism" of the time:

> As many arrows, loosed several ways,
> Come to one mark;
> As many ways meet in one town;
> As many fresh streams meet in one salt sea,
> As many lines close in the dial's center;
> So may a thousand actions, once afoot,
> End in one purpose, and be all well borne.

Some critics detect strong irony in this play. We may note some subtleties which imply irony in this scene. Henry, demanding that Canterbury plunge England into war only with the purest of reasons, says that he himself will

> believe in heart
> That what you speak is in your conscience washed
> As pure as sin with baptism.

What Henry needs is precisely to have the sin he is planning "washed pure."

Later, Canterbury speaks of the past deeds of England, which

> make her chronicle as rich with praise
> As is the ooze and bottom of the sea
> With sunken wreck and sumless treasuries

The incongruity of the image (oozy wrecks as tokens of praise) suggests a twist to the thought.

ACT II · PROLOGUE

Summary
The chorus describes the eagerness of England's preparation for war and the dedication of all Englishmen to Henry,

"the mirror of all Christian kings." He speaks of the French fear of the coming war and of three English traitors, Cambridge, Scroop and Grey, who, bribed into a conspiracy with the French, plan to kill Henry before he sets sail for France. When Henry enters, we are told, the scene will be Southampton, from where the audience will be taken over to France, and back with

> gentle pass. For, if we may,
> We'll not offend one stomach with our play.

Commentary

The vivid poetry of the prologue conveys a colorful picture of England preparing for the service of the hero-king. It also reveals the conspiracy against Henry.

The prologues remind us that we are looking at a play. At the same time, they challenge our imagination to look beyond the stage:

> O England! Model to thy inward greatness,
> Like little body with a mighty heart.

So must the little theater and puny actor embody the great spirit of the country and its king.

There was, of course, a chuckle at the chorus' statement that not a soul would get sea-sick from this crossing of the channel. The phrase is also a pun. To "offend one stomach" also refers to critical taste: one's stomach might be offended by a bad play.

ACT II · SCENE I

Summary

Lieutenant Bardolph, on a London Street outside Mistress Quickly's tavern, tries to pacify Corporal Nym, who is upset with Ancient Pistol for having married Nell Quickly when she was "trothplight" to Nym. (The term *Ancient* refers to a military office Pistol holds, not to his age.) The corporal says, darkly:

Things must be as they may. Men may sleep, and they may have their throats about them at that time, and some say knives have edges. It must be as it may. Though patience be a tired mare, yet she will plod.

Pistol and the hostess come in, and Nym and Pistol exchange abuse and threats. They are stopped from blows only by Bardolph's cry that he'll stab the first that strikes. Falstaff's servant-boy comes with word that his master is very ill. The boy suggests to Bardolph: "Put thy face between his sheets and do the office of a warming pan." The hostess goes inside. Again the two men start to quarrel, Nym demanding the eight shillings he had won from Pistol in a bet. "Base is the slave that pays!" cries Pistol, but again Bardolph threatens to kill the first that strikes a blow, and Pistol says he'll give Nym a noble (six shillings and eight pence) ready cash. They shake hands for brotherhood in the war, where Pistol anticipates good pickings as a camp sutler (one who sells provisions to soldiers). The quarrel over Nell Quickly (now Mistress Pistol) is forgotten. She reappears, summoning them to the dying Falstaff's side. They go lamenting the effect the king's rejection has had upon the knight.

Commentary

The Eastcheap environment shows another side of English life, far different from the courtly chambers we have seen in Act I. Here are the common people, who are swept into the war to serve the purposes of the king, the churchmen and the nobles. Yet all their natures are equally human. The bishops seek to preserve their property, the king wants to add France to his dominions and Pistol looks forward to the war, confident that "profits will accrue."

By seeing some of Prince Hal's former jolly companions and hearing of Falstaff's illness, we are reminded of the low but warm human associations Henry has had to forgo on assuming the crown. We are also prepared for the final departure of Falstaff from the picture.

The language of this scene is both racy and realistic. Shakespeare captures the coarse tones of the street, at the same time adding subtle touches. Both Nym and Pistol misuse the language. Nym says: "That is the rendezvous of it," meaning "the end." He also invents a demon, Barbason. Pistol is more

grandiose. He says of Falstaff: "His heart is fracted and corroborate." He also swells into the inflated rhetoric of earlier Elizabethan drama:

O braggart vile, and damnèd furious wight,
The grave doth gape, and doting death is near.
Therefore exhale!

Despite these comic effects, the scene lacks the full-hearted exuberance of the comic episodes in the Henry IV plays. This is a new world. The comic characters seem bent on nothing but cutting one another's throats; war is in the air; Henry has traded good fellowship for success. This is no world for Falstaff. Into one brief sentence of the hostess, Shakespeare packs the pathos of the change: "The king has killed his heart."

Lieutenant Bardolph has been promoted. In the earlier plays, he was a corporal. The boy's suggestion that Bardolph use his face as a warming pan recalls the ruddy complexion and fiery nose Falstaff had frequently poked fun at, especially in his lengthy description of it in Act III, Scene 3 of *Henry IV*, Part I. *Ancient* Pistol means *Ensign*, second lieutenant. Corporal Nym, a newcomer to the company, is well named; *nym* is Elizabethan slang for *filch* ("steal").

The term, "trothplight," in Elizabethan days might be a tricky matter. If two persons agreed, in the presence of witnesses, to take one another as man and wife, they were legally betrothed, and any other marriage was void. This betrothal was so binding that many couples went through no further ceremony. As a consequence, wealthy widows were particularly plagued by proposals and rapidly remarried. There is a story of a young gentleman who knelt beside a wealthy widow at her late husband's funeral and whispered his proposal, but she responded that she was already pledged. Here, we find Pistol married to Dame Quickly and, therefore, owner of her tavern. Being a soldier, however, he scorns to be thought a tradesman and swears at Bardolph for addressing him as "host."

The tavern, by the way, is not of the highest repute. The hostess agrees with her husband that they will no longer keep lodgers, "for we cannot lodge and board a dozen or fourteen gentlewomen that live honestly by the prick of their needles but it will be thought we keep a bawdy house." Pistol, in his quarrel

with Nym, bids him call their servant, Doll Tearsheet, "from the powdering tub of infamy" and marry her. The *powdering tub* was a place where persons were sweated as a treatment for venereal disease.

Nell Quickly is not the only one who sighs over the fate of Falstaff in this scene. Nym declares, "The king hath run bad humors on the knight," and Pistol (the quarrel ended) agrees: "Nym, thou hast spoke the right."

ACT II · SCENE 2

Summary

The Dukes of Exeter and Bedford and the Earl of Westmoreland know of the conspiracy announced in the prologue and are concerned that the king should trust himself with the traitors. The king enters almost at once, followed by the very men in question — the Earl of Cambridge, Lord Scroop and Sir Thomas Grey. Henry is confident of success in France and extracts from each of the three traitors lavish predictions of triumph and assurances of the entire kingdom's loyalty. Thanking them, he promises to reward each of his subjects according to his worth.

Commanding the Duke of Exeter to set free a man arrested the day before for treasonous language against himself, Henry explains that the poor fellow was irresponsible on account of drunkenness. All three of the traitors protest against this show of lenience as dangerous. They advise that the man should be executed or, at least, tortured and imprisoned.

Expecting to be appointed commissioners to govern England during the king's absence, each then receives a parchment from the king, which, when he reads it, each finds to be a detailed statement of his guilt as a conspirator, charging him with having received gold for the purpose from France. Having trapped the three into pronouncing their own death sentences, Henry upbraids them in a calm and restrained manner, but showing bitterness beneath at having been in each case not only betrayed by a subject but a close friend. The traitors are then removed to their execution.

The king immediately turns his attention to the departure for France.

Commentary

Henry's character and the ideal of kingship that he represents are more fully revealed. The scene also demonstrates his efficiency and competence as he deals with the traitors.

Henry V is taking his place in the grand picture of succession Shakespeare is presenting throughout his history plays. The present conspiracy is reminiscent of those with which Henry's father, Henry IV, had to contend. The problems of the father descend to the son. The war will occupy the minds of the feuding factions that remained after the death of Henry IV, as the old king foresaw on this deathbed (*Henry IV*, Part II, Act IV, Scene 5, 211-214):

> Therefore, my Harry,
> Be it thy course to busy giddy minds
> With foreign quarrels; that action, hence borne out,
> May waste the memory of the former days.

This scene of conspiracy also serves to remind us of another problem that the reigning king inherited from his father. When we learn of three Englishmen who plan to take his life, we cannot help but recall the illegal deposition of Richard II by which Henry IV took the throne. From this illegality sprang the great insecurity Henry IV felt throughout his reign, as well as his overwhelming psychological need to know that his line was safely established on the throne. To him, this knowledge would be a sign that his great sin against God in deposing His lawful representative, Richard, had been forgiven. This dynastic insecurity, inherited from his father, provides Henry's strongest motivation in seeking the conquest of France and explains his constant need to find justification for his actions and someone else to blame for any questionable deed.

Henry's long speech condemning the conspirators is largely Shakespeare's original; it differs widely from Holinshed. In it, Shakespeare studies the idea of kingship. In his condemnation of him, Henry lists qualities he says he had thought to have been Scroop's. Actually, they characterize the ideal aristocrat: dutiful, learned, religious, temperate, constant, controlling passion with reason and ruling sense with judgment. This is similar to the ideal that Shakespeare develops elsewhere, as when Antony describes Brutus at the end of *Julius Caesar* and when

Hamlet describes Horatio. As Theodore Spencer says in *Shakespeare and the Nature of Man*:

> It is the ideal of the whole Hellenistic tradition of the nature of man, whose specific function, reason, should govern the passions which spring from the senses he shares with animals, those beings below him in Nature's hierarchy to whose level he tends only too easily to fall.

This was the ideal that Henry strove to achieve.

Henry, however, was well aware of the all-too-human reality that lies beneath the appearance of perfection, as this very scene illustrates. Henry has skilfully manipulated the situation to allow himself to display some of the inspiring qualities of a public hero. He shows courage in allowing the conspiracy to progress this far. The courage, however, is not nearly so careless as it seems, since his generals know of the plot and the king is well-protected. Henry has contrived, by tricking these personal enemies into advising him to show no mercy to traitors, to send them to their deaths justifiably. By emphasizing the personal affection he has for these men, he shows he is able to subdue emotion. He rises above his impulse to show mercy to the men he loved. And by submitting these traitors to the law of the land, he does his duty as king. The charge against them all is that they have accepted French gold to betray England. But Cambridge says:

> For me, the gold of France did not seduce,
> Although I did admit it as a motive
> The sooner to effect what I intended —

He was moved by other ambition, for he had the same sort of claim, through a woman, to the throne of England as Henry had to the throne of France.

This scene demonstrates that Henry is a champion at, among other things, putting his opponents in the wrong.

ACT II · SCENE 3

Summary

The fact that the hostess wishes to accompany her husband to Staines, sixteen miles west of London on the Thames (first leg

of the march to Southampton) shows that this scene precedes Scene 2 in point of time. Its main interest lies in the hostess' description of the death of Sir John Falstaff. This is a famous literary gem, human and very touching in its artless sincerity, enhanced by the misuse of English by a simple, uneducated woman. The pathetic details of Falstaff's end are moving. Bardolph is particularly affected, mainly because he has now lost the chief source of his supply of drink.

Pistol refuses to let Nell accompany him to Staines, apparently because he is grieving for Falstaff, kisses her and gives her some very unnecessary advice about her personal conduct and the management of the inn while he is away. He invites Bardolph to kiss her good-bye and he does so. Nym refuses to do so out of jealousy, and the three confederate rascals are off, accompanied by the boy as their servant.

Commentary

Coming right after the treason of the high-ranking nobles, the personal motives of the commoners are shown as equally dishonorable: "to suck, to suck, the very blood to suck!" The death of Falstaff ends the frequently slapstick and rough, but warm-hearted and irresponsible, comedy of the Henry IV plays.

Shakespeare endows the earthy description of Falstaff's death — although it has its obscene moments — with a tender pathos that gives a deeper tone to the drama.

In the epilogue to *Henry IV*, Part II, there is a promise: "If you be not too much cloyed with fat meat [i.e., Falstaff] our humble author will continue the story, with Sir John in it." Sir John Falstaff was tremendously popular; why then do we not see him in *Henry V*? One theory states that he was indeed included in an early version of the play, that he went to France and that it was Falstaff, not Pistol, who was forced to eat the leek in Act V, Scene 1. He was, the story goes, then removed because of the protests of the Brooke family, the descendants of Oldcastle, the man many believed was the real-life counterpart to the fat knight. This account, however, does not hold water for, had the family this power and this desire, they would have rooted the fat knight out of all three plays. Other reasons have been suggested. Some scholars point out that Will Kempe, who probably played Falstaff, had left the company. Others wonder whether Shakespeare had exhausted that vein of humor; the

Falstaff that later turns up in *The Merry Wives of Windsor* has all of the bulk, but little of the warm humor and bouncing wit, of the earlier Sir John. The most obvious reason, whatever degree of truth may lie in other theories, is that Falstaff and Henry V, after the outright rejection of the knight, cannot come face to face. There is no room for the jolly prankster in King Henry's rigid world. With Falstaff's death, that human, carefree quality in Prince Hal is buried.

Samuel Johnson made a shrewd observation in his suggestion that Shakespeare killed the popular Falstaff in order that "no other writer might attempt to exhibit him." As to the promise that Falstaff would be shown again, Johnson remarks: "It is dangerous to sell the bear when it is not yet hunted."

When the hostess declares that Falstaff is not in Hell, but in "Arthur's bosom," she is confusing the early English heroic King Arthur with the early Hebrew leader, Abraham.

One passage of the hostess' description of the dying Falstaff reads: "and a' babbled of green fields." The passage shows the dying knight, a city man if ever there was one, in his last moments touchingly thinking back to the countryside of his boyhood. The First Folio reading is "and a Table of green fields," which seems not to make sense. It has been ingeniously argued, however, that the original is correct. A *table*, among other things, might mean a tablet or sign, as that in front of a tavern, and the dying Falstaff who "cried out of sack," may have been thinking of a place where he enjoyed it.

Pistol's advice to his wife, who stays behind in charge of the tavern while he goes to seek profit in the war, neatly sets the pattern of morality in the play:

Let senses rule, the word is "Pitch and Pay."
Trust none;
For oaths are straws, men's faiths are wafer-cakes,
And Hold-fast is the only dog, my duck.

Even in the talk of the companion they have just lost, Shakespeare adds a realistic note of bitterness. Reference is made to Bardolph's red nose, and Bardolph at once retorts: "'Well, the fuel is gone that maintained that fire. That's all the riches I got in his service." They turn then to thoughts of the war with France, and this bitter exclamation is the last allusion

to Falstaff, except when Fluellen (Act IV, Scene 7), speaking of the fat knight, says, "I have forgot his name."

ACT II · SCENE 4

Summary

The French king, meeting with his council to consider the English threat, hears the dauphin belittle Henry and the Constable of France warn the dauphin that he is in error, Henry being marvellously changed. The king reminds them of the English victory at Crécy and declares they must make strong preparation.

Exeter is announced as ambassador from England. He tells the king that Henry, as descendant of Edward III, has fair claim to the French throne. If it is not resigned to him, the French will be guilty of shedding the blood of their countrymen. Exeter then delivers a message of scorn to the dauphin. For Henry, he contemptuously returns the prince's rude joke and says all France shall weep because of it. The dauphin flings back defiance. The French king promises to answer the next day. Exeter tells him to deliver the message with all speed, as Henry has already set foot on the soil of France.

Commentary

The enemy are shown in their concern over the English invasion. While the dauphin still regards Henry lightly, the Constable of France has heard of Henry's reformation. The king is also worried over the power of the English.

The Salic Law (which states that the crown can pass only through male inheritance) discussed in Act 1, Scene 2, and which is the major obstacle to the claim England makes to the French throne, was upheld when Philip V of France succeeded his brother, Charles IV. Their sister, Isabella, had married Edward II of England and their son, Edward III, recognized as king of France by the Holy Roman Emperor, went to war to gain the French throne. His son, Edward, the Black Prince, was victorious at the Battle of Crécy, August 26, 1346, at which ten thousand Englishmen armed with the long bow defeated twenty thousand French crossbowmen and undisciplined cavalry. It is therefore not surprising, when Exeter brings up the name of

Edward III in renewing the English claim, that the French king is troubled. Exeter is following Henry's pattern and, we may assume, Henry's instructions in telling the French that if they do not surrender, the guilt of the consequent destruction will fall on them.

In the midst of the high-vaulting phrases and resounding words of the nobility, it is interesting to note Shakespeare's use of homely images drawn from the everyday activities of common men. Thus, the Constable of France speaks of Henry's apparently careless youth:

> Covering discretion with a coat of folly;
> As gardeners do with ordure hide those roots
> That shall first spring and be most delicate.

And the dauphin admits that it is better to overestimate the strength of an enemy:

> So the proportions of defence are filled,
> Which of a weak and niggardly projection
> Doth, like a miser, spoil his coat with scanting
> A little cloth.

The dauphin speaks of the tennis balls he sent Henry as "the Paris balls." Roy Battenhouse declares that "the whole play, in its undertones, is a splendid contest between London gunstones and Paris balls; between Greeks with an Achilles heel and Trojan Paris-lovers (the pun in Act II, Scene 4, 132) with their Nell; between Ares and Aphrodite . . . ." And indeed there is indelicate talk in the tavern, on the battlefield and in court.

ACT III • PROLOGUE

Summary

The chorus asks us to imagine the English fleet, "a city on the inconstant billows dancing," bearing the choicest sons of England to the war. We are to imagine Harfleur surrounded and besieged. Word has come that the French king offers Henry

> Katherine his daughter, and with her to dowry,
> Some petty and unprofitable dukedoms.
> The offer likes not.

The cannon resounds; the battle is on.

Commentary

The prologue bridges time — and the British Channel. It tells us the terms of the French king's peace offer and of Henry's rejection of them.

Again, the admission of the limitations of the stage permits Shakespeare to insert pictures he could not otherwise give:

> Play with your fancies, and in them behold
> Upon the hempen tackle shipboys climbing.
> Hear the shrill whistle that doth order give
> To sounds confused . . .
>   . . . . Still be kind,
> And eke out our performance with your mind.

Harfleur, just east of the present Le Havre at the mouth of the Seine, was, in Henry's time, a major port of France and an avenue to Paris. It was captured in this siege and held by the English for twenty years, until Henry's son, Henry VI, lost it in 1535.

ACT III · SCENE 1

Summary

This scene provides a sample of the inspiring personal leadership of Henry. It contains a fighting speech calculated to stir the spirits of these men he knows so well, an appeal to their pride in themselves, in their ancestry, in their country. Amid his battleleaders, and surrounded with soldiers carrying scaling-ladders, he calls for one more supreme effort. He rouses that sporting, fighting spirit characteristic of the English then as now.

Standing before the walls of Harfleur, King Henry exhorts his troops to take the city. He addresses, at first, the entire army. Then he speaks directly to the nobles:

> Dishonor not your mothers; now attest
> That those whom you called fathers did beget you.

Finally, he calls upon the yeomen:

> Whose limbs were made in England, show us here
> The mettle of your pasture. Let us swear

That you were worth your breeding; which I doubt
     not,
For there is none of you so mean and base
That hath not noble luster in your eyes.

Then he concludes:

I see you stand like greyhounds in the slips,
Straining upon the start. The game's afoot!
Follow your spirit; and upon this charge
Cry "God for Harry, England and Saint George!"

Commentary

The ideal king is here shown at his best, as an inspiring leader. Henry's thirty-four lines constitute the most inspiriting rallying speech in all literature.

Even today, this speech never seems to fail in stirring patriotism in English hearts. Henry's words before Harfleur were the most frequently quoted speech on the British Broadcasting Corporation's airwaves during World War II.

It is unusual for an entire scene to consist of just one speech. The moment of its delivery, often staged with Henry standing above his troops on inclined planks running up to the breach on the Harfleur wall, gives it added emphasis. Then, following their heroic leader, the troops dash into the fight.

Note again the appearance of animal images in the talk of war. "Now set the teeth and stretch the nostril wide" reminds us of horses. The men are told to "imitate the action of the tiger." The yeomen have come from their "pasture." The greyhounds are impatient, and "the game's afoot."

ACT III · SCENE 2

Summary

After the lofty spirit of Henry's rallying speech, we have a glimpse of the opposite spirit. We see our familiar three cowardly rogues hanging back and letting the other fellows do the work. Bardolph pretends to be inspired by Henry's call to action and makes a show of driving the others to the breach. Knowing him, they do not stir and are very frank in saying they do not want to get killed. Captain Fluellen happens to pass by

and compels them to go forward. The boy remains, for he is a non-combatant, and gives a description of the rascality and cowardice of the three. He adds that because they are trying to make a pickpocket of him he will leave their service.

Fluellen returns and is met by Captain Gower, who is also a Welshman, sent by the Duke of Gloucester to order Fluellen to come to the mining operations to speak to him. Fluellen, displeased that the duke has given the direction of the mining to Captain MacMorris, bitterly criticizes the operation. The mines are too near the surface and have already been countermined by the enemy.

Captain MacMorris enters, accompanied by captain Jamy, a Scot. Ignoring MacMorris, an Irishman, Fluellen praises Jamy to his face as a man steeped in the Roman theory of war. Mac-Morris has a grievance because a parley has been called and he is not going to be able to use his mines to blow up the walls of Harfleur. Fluellen tries to pick an argument with MacMorris to show up his ignorance, but the latter will not be drawn into an argument; the day is too hot and, besides, there is work to be done. Jamy would like to see an argument. Fluellen makes the mistake of remarking that few Irishmen — but he gets no further because MacMorris attacks him with Celtic fury, stung by the sneer in the two words "few Irishmen," and calls him everything he can think of. Fluellen is calm, but again infuriates MacMorris by insisting that he is as good a man as MacMorris. The quarrel is on the brink of swordplay, but Gower intervenes. However, it is the sounding of the parley which prevents action. Fluellen gets in the last word by promising to resume the argument at the first opportunity.

Commentary

After the king's rousing summons to the attack, we are shown other aspects of army activity: the cowardice and dishonesty of a few non-commissioned officers and the petty disputes of the captains over strategy. The sense of diversity is strengthened by having captains representing the four divisions of the British Isles — England, Ireland, Scotland and Wales.

The humor Shakespeare extracted from Pistol and Bardolph in the earlier Henry plays is growing thin. Here they are no longer amusing but contemptible, squirming out of the fight and committing petty theft. We are being prepared for their

shabby end. "Their villainy," says the boy, "goes against my weak stomach, and therefore I must cast it up."

Pistol cannot help being talkative. He has, as the boy neatly observes, "a killing tongue and a quiet sword." But the boy puts the common feeling about war into a sentence that, coming from a mere lad, has both vigor and pathos: "Would I were in an alehouse in London! I would give all my fame for a pot of ale and safety." There upon Pistol breaks into song:

> If wishes would prevail with me,
> My purpose should not fail with me,
> But thither I would hie.

He masks his cowardice with music. It is at this moment that Fluellen appears and drives them to the battle.

ACT III · SCENE 3

Summary

The parley is held. It begins with a long speech by Henry, who swears that if the half-taken city does not surrender, he will allow his soldiers to ravage and plunder. He threatens:

> Your fresh-fair virgins and your flow'ring infants.
> . . . .
> your shrill-shrieking daughters;
> Your naked infants spitted upon pikes,
> Whiles the mad mothers and their howls confused
> Do break the clouds, as did the wives of Jewry
> At Herod's bloody-hunting slaughtermen.

Moreover, since it was the practice of war, if a city refused to yield and then was taken, to loose the soldiers upon the citizens, Henry, as usual, could wash his hands of responsibility and call his conscience clean:

> What is't to me, when you yourselves are cause,
> If your pure maidens fall into the hand
> Of hot and forcing violation?

The governor of Harfleur responds that the city's hopes have failed. The dauphin has sent word that his forces are not ready to retaliate:

> Therefore, great king,
> We yield our town and lives to your soft mercy.

Henry leaves Exeter in charge, with orders to strengthen the fortifications and to "use mercy to them all." He says, as winter is coming on, he will retire to Calais.

Commentary

The king is revealed as ferocious if opposed, but, if his terms are met, merciful — another quality of the ideal king. The war is advanced by the taking of Harfleur.

The animal imagery continues. Henry speaks of "the fleshed soldier," *fleshed* meaning roused by the taste of blood.

The king's mention of "the wives of Jewry" is an allusion to the Slaughter of the Innocents (*Matthew*, 2) when Herod, angry because his wise men did not reveal to him where they had found the infant Jesus, ordered the death of all the male children in Bethlehem and in all that region who were two years old or under. It is another of the play's many subtle ironies that Henry, protesting that his conscience is clear, should use images that point to evil. He declares that the soldier, "In liberty of bloody hand shall range with conscience wide as Hell," and he compares the lamenting at his "innocent" acts with the Bible's "wailing and loud lamentation" over Herod's most guilty deed.

ACT III · SCENE 4

Summary

In the French king's palace, Princess Katherine asks her attendant, Alice, who has been to England, to teach her the language. Neither can pronounce English well, but Katherine asks for and learns the words *hand*, *fingers*, *nails*, *arm*, *elbow*, *neck*, *chin*, *foot* and *gown*. When she hears the last two words Katherine protests that she will never speak them before the lords of France, for the words are coarse and naughty. Nevertheless, she repeats her lesson and then says that's enough for one time.

Commentary

This scene gives us a break from the sterner atmosphere of war, with a light, amusing conversation between the first noblewomen we have seen in the play. The princess learns some words, the sounds of which, innocent in English, make words in French that in her day were not spoken in polite society. The scene shows Katherine aware of, and preparing for, her role as part of the prize Henry may take back from France.

This scene, except for the poorly pronounced English words Katherine is learning, is entirely in French. Some scholars suggest that Shakespeare may have learned the language while lodging in Cripplegate Ward, London, with the Huguenot wigmaker Christopher Montjoy. Montjoy's attractive daughter, Mary, it is thought, taught the playwright French. We learn about Shakespeare's residence there from the paper filed in a suit in 1612, when Stephen Belott sued for payment of the dowry promised when he married Mary — a promise William Shakespeare, as a witness at the betrothal, was summoned to confirm. (Notice that the French herald in the play is named Montjoy.) It is also reasonable to assume that Shakespeare would not have inserted this scene of sixty-four lines, all in French, if some general acquaintance with that tongue were not within the range of most of the London audience.

It is commonly asserted that the First Folio printers made hash of the French in this scene, and various editors have altered it to their taste. William Warburton, in his 1747 edition of the play, said: "I have left this ridiculous scene as I found it," but he wished he could have deleted it as some other writer's insertion. Samuel Johnson declared:

> The scene is indeed mean enough when it is read, but the grimaces of two French women and the odd accent with which they uttered the English made it divert upon the stage . . . . The Princess suspects no deficiency in her instructress, nor the instructress in herself. Throughout the whole scene there may be found French servility and French vanity.

When Johnson wrote this in 1765, the English had just defeated the French in the Seven Years' War.

Roy Battenhouse protests that this scene, far from being irrelevant, may be pivotal. It is set between the scene of the images of rape at Harfleur and that of the French warriors' indecent discussion of the barbarous English. Katherine who has already been offered to Henry, is preparing herself for the match. The words she asks about suggest, as Battenhouse observes, "a progress in love-making" that omits the heart. Beginning with the hand, she moves up the arm to the neck and chin ("as if for a stolen kiss"), then swiftly down with bilingual puns to more fundamental things. And the princess consistently pronounces the English *chin* as *sin*.

Katherine's beginning with the hand seems further relevant, Battenhouse points out. Twice it occurs in Henry's speech in the previous scene: "the hand of hot and forcing violation . . . . the blind and bloody soldier with foul hand." MacMorris regularly swears "By my hand." At the play's end, Pistol intends to make thievish use of his "quick hand." Thus Katherine's concern with the hand and its parts may allude, not only to the cold calculation of her political marriage, but to the stretching out of Henry's grasping hand toward the throne of France.

A further subtlety may lie in the "fractured French" of the First Folio. Katherine asks the English word for "le main," which is masculine. But the French word is feminine; it should be "la main." Perhaps Shakespeare wanted the audience to hear French *main* and English *man* — the sound is almost the same. Then Katherine's question would contain, as underthought, the pun: "What is the man (Henry) in English?" And the answer comes: "The man is called the hand."

In another transferred sound, Katherine confuses "nails" with "males." Later on (Act IV, Scene 4, 75), we hear mention of the nails of the "roaring devil i' the old play." Thus, the French may think of the English as men with claws.

Even if one considers some of these subtleties beyond Shakespeare's intention, or beyond the understanding of his audience, it should be clear that his farcical scenes do more than merely provide entertainment or comic relief. In various lighter ways, they reinforce the play's underlying and almost hidden theme, that of the claw clutching and the hand grasping for power.

ACT III · SCENE 5

Summary

This scene at the French court presents a strange mixture of shame and contempt, over-confidence and apprehension. It shows divided counsels, laxity of behavior and insufferable pride. It also shows the dauphin insubordinate and rude.

Two months after Harfleur, Henry has found a bridge to cross the Somme at Péronne on his way to Calais, then an English possession, where he can quarter his sick troops and be close to England for fresh supplies and reinforcements. The Constable of France declares that Henry must be fought at once or there will be no living in France. The dauphin is still contemptuous of the English. The dauphin reluctantly admits, though, that the women of France are beginning to look to the English for lovers. Bretagne is angry at the English insult that the French agility in retreat ought make them eligible for English dancing schools.

The king suddenly orders all the nobility to the front, but orders the dauphin to remain at home with him. The dauphin practically refuses. The king pleads with him to obey.

Commentary

In this scene, we are shown the resolution of the French and their contempt for the barbarous English. We may be reminded of the saying "Pride goeth before a fall."

Referring to the Englishmen as "bastard Normans" is a reminder that they were descended from the followers of William the Conqueror, a Norman, who defeated the Saxon English in 1066 and knighted many of his followers on the battlefield. The dauphin, in an elaborate metaphor compares these Norman French to slips for grafting, which, set upon the wild English branches, seem to have grown larger than the cultivated trees from which they were taken.

An amusing but well-known description of England comes from the Duke of Bourbon when he exclaims that, if the English march is not met by the French forces,

> I will sell my dukedom
> To buy a slobbery and a dirty farm
> In that nook-shotten isle of Albion.

"Nook-shotten" means "running out into corners." Albion, another name for England, means "the white land," so called from the chalk cliffs of Dover overhanging the English coast.

The ladies' scornful thought that the French should teach dancing because their grace is in their heels of course puns upon the notion that when the English approach, the French take to their heels. Putting this accusation of cowardice into the mouths of the French is more effective and more forceful than having it uttered by the English.

ACT III · SCENE 6

Summary

Fluellen, at the English camp in Picardy, is telling Gower that Exeter has admirably held the bridge and that he had there a gallant assistant. The man in question, Pistol, comes in and begs Fluellen to do him a favor:

> Bardolph, a soldier, firm and sound of heart,
> And of buxom valor, hath by cruel fate
> And giddy Fortune's furious fickle wheel,
> That goddess blind
> That stands upon the rolling restless stone, —

Fluellen interrupts, with almost equal wordiness, to expound on Fortune having a wheel and standing upon a rolling stone. But when he hears that Bardolph has stolen a pax (a holy tablet) and is to be hanged and that Pistol wants him to plead for mercy, Fluellen says that, to maintain discipline, he would let even his own brother die. Pistol goes off cursing — "Figo for thy friendship!" — and Gower tells Fluellen that Pistol is a fool and a rogue. Many such, he says, go to war, learn all the details of the fighting, let their beards grow like the general's and make great profit of it at home "among foaming bottles and ale-washed wits." Fluellen promises to give Pistol a piece of his mind.

King Henry comes in, and Fluellen reports Exeter's success in holding the bridge. The enemy's loss has been "very great, reasonable great." The English have lost only Bardolph, who is to be executed for robbing a church. "His face is all bubukles, and whelks, and knobs, and flames o' fire. And his lips plows

at his nose, and it is like a coal of fire, sometimes plue and sometimes red; but his nose is executed, and his fire's out." Henry orders that all such offenders be put to death and that there be no pillaging by his soldiers as they march. "For when lenity and cruelty play for a kingdom, the gentler gamester is the soonest winner."

The herald, Montjoy, arrives with the French king's message. He asks Henry to

> consider of his ransom . . . . For our losses, his exchequer is too poor. For the effusion of our blood, the muster of his kingdom too faint a number. And for our disgrace, his own person, kneeling at our feet, but a weak and worthless satisfaction. To this add defiance. And tell him, for conclusion, he hath betrayed his followers, whose condemnation is pronounced.

Henry answers with calm dignity. He admits that his army is weakened and diminished by sickness, and his remaining soldiers "almost no better than so many French." He tells Montjoy:

> Go therefore tell your master here I am.
> My ransom is this frail and worthless trunk . . . .
> Yet, God before, tell him we will come on,
> Though France himself and such another neighbor
> Stand in our way.

Henry gives the herald a purse for his labor and then orders the army to encamp beyond the bridge.

Commentary

Before the blows of battle, it was customary for the leaders to exchange words. Both do this with appropriate dignity. Now we expect the fight.

In the meantime, the disintegration of Falstaff's old company continues.

Pistol says Bardolph has stolen a *pax*; Holinshed records that a soldier stole a *pyx* and the king had him strangled. A pax is a tablet stamped with a crucifix, to be kissed by the celebrating priest at Mass. A pyx is a vessel in which the con-

secrated bread of the Sacrament is kept. To steal either of these is not only theft but sacrilege, and would, of course, increase the hostility of the plundered countryfolk toward Henry's soldiers.

Although Bardolph is named and vividly described, Henry shows no sign of recognizing his old companion. Fluellen speaks the rogue's brief epitaph: "His fire's out."

Gower's words about begging or cheating soldiers who copy the general's beard may be an allusion to Essex, who, after his Cadiz expedition, grew a great beard which was widely imitated by Elizabethans. Some scholars state that Shakespeare had Essex much in mind at this time. The leniency Henry exercises after Harfleur, for instance, is not historically true of Henry, but is true of Essex in his Continental wars. There is an unmistakable allusion to Essex in the prologue to Act V.

The proud Welshman, Fluellen, is full of ancient parallels. He here compares the Duke of Exeter to Agamemnon, legendary leader of the Greeks against Troy. Later, he likens Henry to the historical Greek conqueror, "Alexander the Pig" (Fluellen's mispronunciation of *Big*; the phrase is his term for Alexander the Great). His quarrel with MacMorris was over the way he thought the Romans waged their wars. Note that the Welshman's accent causes him to mispronounce several words, especially those beginning with *b* or *g*.

ACT III · SCENE 7

Summary

Near Agincourt, the dauphin and other leaders of the French army are passing the night hours in idle boasting. The dauphin grows extravagant in praise of his riding horse: "My horse is my mistress." The Constable of France, who has grown tired of the dauphin's self-indulgent words, counters:

Con: I had as lief have my mistress a jade.
Dau: I tell thee, Constable, my mistress wears his own hair.
Con: I could make as true a boast as that if I had a sow to my mistress.
Dau: "Le chien est retourné a son propre vomisse-

ment, et la truie lavée au bourbier." [The dog
is returned to his own vomit and the washed
sow to the mire.]

Lord Rambures interrupts the quarrel by offering to toss
dice for twenty prisoners. It being midnight, the dauphin leaves
to prepare his armor. Then Rambures remarks: "He longs to
eat the English" and the still annoyed Constable of France
retorts: "I think he will eat all he kills." Orleans takes the
dauphin's part. Then the talk turns to the "wretched and
peevish" king of England "with his fat-brained followers." The
French laugh at their enemies, who are rough as mastiffs, "leaving their wits and their wives. And then give them great meals of
beef, and iron and steel, they will eat like wolves, and fight like
devils." "Aye," says Orleans, "but these English are shrewdly
out of beef." It being now two o'clock, they go to arm
themselves, expecting that

by ten
We shall have each a hundred Englishmen.

Commentary

We are shown the French, frivolous and overconfident in
this scene that takes place on the eve of the battle.

Again, there is talk of animals. There are references to
wolves, bearbaiting and the English mastiffs, "foolish curs, that
run winking into the mouth of a Russian bear and have their
heads crushed like rotten apples." There are some obscene allusions and wordplay in the talk of horses and mistresses. Then
the dauphin cites scripture for his purpose. The French quotation is from Peter II: 2-22: "The dog is returned to his own
vomit, and the sow that was washed, to her wallowing in the
mire." The incongruity between the source of the quotation and
the occasion of its use adds to the emptiness of the conversation
and to our feeling that the French commanders lack any sense
of the values at stake.

Shakespeare adds at least a semblance of action by having
the officers of each army quarrel among themselves. The
English, note, argue over questions of military strategy; the
French, over the values of horses and mistresses.

ACT IV · PROLOGUE

Summary

The chorus describes how in the night each army hears the other moving about: the clanging made by the armorers, the challenging neigh of horses and, almost, the passwords of the enemy sentinels:

> The confident and overlusty French
> Do the low-rated English play at dice,
> And chide the cripple tardy-gaited night
> Who like a foul and ugly witch doth limp
> So tediously away. The poor condemnèd English,
> Like sacrifices, by their watchful fires
> Sit patiently and inly ruminate
> The morning's danger.

But the king, walking about the camp with a fresh face and a cheery word for knight and yeoman alike, cheers up the dispirited army and rouses them with "A little touch of Harry in the night." Then, with one more apology for the insufficiency of the stage, the chorus announces the Battle of Agincourt.

Commentary

Since we have seen the French offering to throw dice for English prisoners and shall in a moment see Henry walking through his camp, the prologue carries no essential news. But it serves a double purpose. First, it adds description of the scene that the bare stage cannot provide and, second, it continues the emphasis on Henry as the ideal leader, mingling with and inspiring his men:

>   Oh, now who will behold
> The royal captain of this ruined band
> Walking from watch to watch, from tent to tent,
> Let him cry "Praise and glory on his head!"

ACT IV · SCENE 1

Summary

It is nighttime in the English camp. The king is admitting to his brother, Gloucester, that their situation is perilous.

However, they do have advantages over the French. For instance, the enemy teaches them to rise earlier, and that is the way to wealth. Sir Thomas Erpingham happens by, and Henry on an impulse borrows his cloak and sends the others on to gather the lords together in his tent. He is now unrecognizable to most as the king.

Pistol enters, challenges the disguised king in characteristic extravagant manner, reveals a patriotic attachment to the king's person and asks his name. He is satisfied with the answer, Harry le Roy. But when he finds out that his unknown acquaintance is a Welshman and a friend of Fluellen's, he sends a message to the latter that he will knock his leek about his head on St. David's Day, the Welsh national holiday. Henry warns him that he may get knocked about the head, too. Pistol exits and Henry steps back a bit into the shadow. Fluellen and Gower meet. Fluellen criticizes Gower at great length for speaking the words, "Captain Fluellen" too loudly in front of the enemy. When Gower gets a chance, he objects that the enemy is making just as much noise. Fluellen pours another avalanche of reproach over him. To cut this disagreement off before morning, Gower agrees, "I will speak lower." When they are gone Henry remarks to himself that Fluellen is a good soldier, if somewhat quaint.

Three soldiers, Bates, Court and Williams, enter. Williams challenges Henry. Henry replies he is serving under Sir John Erpingham when he should have said Sir Thomas. This may be an error, or it may be a test by Henry to see whether they know better than that. They do not, at any rate.

Bates and Henry discuss whether the king should be informed of their desperate situation. Henry says he should not be for, being only a man, he might show fear and thereby dishearten the army. Bates would like to be out of this war. The king could stay and be ransomed, he suggests. Henry says he is sure Bates would not like to leave the king alone.

Williams is not sure the king's course is just. Bates interrupts to say that their duty is to fight for the king. If the king's cause is wrong, their duty wipes out any blame on their part. Williams suggests that those who die in battle unconfessed will be laid at the king's door. The king replies that everyone should be at war and go into battle confessed and with sins forgiven, or better still, live a good life. But the king is not responsible for

their deaths, anyway; all he intended was the use of their services.

The king returns to the idea that he could be ransomed while the whole army was killed and says that he himself heard the king say he would not be ransomed. Williams, the fifteenth-century comic, says that when they were dead the king might be ransomed and they would be none the wiser. The king replies that, if he lives to see it, he will never trust the king's word again. Williams dismisses this as a foolish remark. When the king intimates that in other circumstances he might be angry at that reply, Williams insists on challenging him to a fight if they both live. Henry accepts and they exchange gloves to wear in their caps to know each other after the battle. Bates, a solid old English type, tells them to be friends, calls them fools and says there are Frenchmen enough to fight.

When they are gone, Henry delivers his famous soliloquy on the tendency of all people to blame the king and the emptiness of the state that surrounds a king for everything that happens to them. His theme is that even a slave has a happier life than the king because, although the former's is full of toil, he sleeps soundly at night, while the king does not on account of cares of state. As Hamlet did in one of his soliloquies, and as Henry himself did in *Henry IV,* Part I, he is justifying himself for being a king at all.

Erpingham finds Henry and tells him his council is looking for him all over the camp. Henry tells him to round them up and he will be there in a minute. Alone again, he utters a heartfelt prayer, which reveals a sense of his father's guilt toward Richard II. He has made what reparation he can and pleads with God not to punish him this day for his father's sin.

Commentary

We are here shown other aspects of Henry as the ideal leader, walking through the camp, spurring on his men and putting the victory in the hands of God. At the same time, we observe once more the prickings of his conscience, now with a double barb, for his responsibility for the war, which will cost so many lives and, as his father's heir, for his share of guilt in the possession of the crown his father took.

Neither Henry's going through the camp in disguise nor his long soliloquy is mentioned in the chronicles. Both are additions of Shakespeare's.

Careful readers will observe flaws in Henry's reasoning, if not actual self-deceit. He states that no king, "be his cause never so spotless . . . can try it out with all unspotted soldiers." Therefore, he continues, these sinful soldiers cannot lay their misdeeds upon the king. He neglects to mention the soldiers that may be "unspotted," yet die and leave widows and orphans to destitution. Even more, he does not consider the problem of the king's responsibility in case his cause is not "spotless" — as indeed Henry's was not because his reasons for entering the war were open to serious question. Thus, his discussion with the three soldiers is questionable rather than sound. His soliloquy ends with an almost bare bit of false pleading when he says that the common people little know "what watch the king keeps to maintain the peace." Yet he has *deliberately* led them into war, a war of foreign conquest. This sort of reasoning, however, seems to ease Henry's conscience, for he uses it when alone with God.

The responsibility of a king for the justice of his wars and the duty of the soldier to obey his sovereign were questions raised in Elizabethan England, especially after Sir William Stanley, in 1587, surrendered the Dutch town of Deventer to the Spanish. Stanley considered England's help to the Netherlands against Spain unjust. Cardinal Allen, in *The Copie of a Letter Written by M. Doctor Allen: Concerning the Yielding Up Of the Citie of Daventrie, Unto his Catholic Majesty, by Sir William Stanley, Knight,* defended Stanley, and King Henry's answer to the soldiers seeks to refute some of the points made by the cardinal. Henry's conclusion is that the soldier must obey the king but, as an individual, he is answerable to God.

Those who see irony in Shakespeare's picture of Henry point to the first of his prayer:

O God of battles, steel my soldiers' hearts!

Henry seems to be substituting Mars, the pagan god of war, for Jesus. God is not *of* but *above* the battle, and God's purpose is not to harden men's hearts but, by His grace, to soften them.

It is an amusing touch of psychology that starts the quarrel between the disguised Henry and Williams. The soldiers wonder whether the king will offer ransom, but Henry says he himself heard the king declare that he would not allow it. "Aye,"

responds Williams, "he said so to make us fight cheerfully. But when our throats are cut, he may be ransomed and we none the wiser." Henry then says: "If I live to see it, I will never trust his word after." The idea of a common soldier's holding it up as a punishment that he will not trust the king's word naturally seems ludicrous to Williams, who observes, "Come, 'tis a foolish saying." Henry, annoyed, reacts, not as a soldier, but as a king: "Your reproof is something too round." A few more words and they exchange gloves as a challenge after the battle.

Shakespeare's use of imagery is admirably varied. Sometimes an image lies, like an iceberg, mainly below the surface, as in lines 20-23:

> And when the mind is quickened, out of doubt,
> The organs, though defunct and dead before,
> Break up their drowsy grave and newly move,
> With casted slough and fresh legerity.

Here, the one word *slough* ties the picture of the mental process to the condition of the snake before and after it has shed its skin.

ACT IV · SCENE 2

Summary

To the dauphin, Orleans and other French leaders comes the Constable of France, telling them the English are waiting for battle. He describes the pitiable condition of the little band of English. Even the French servingmen and peasants, he says, could overcome them. Another French lord, Grandpré, comes in. He adds that the English horses are ready to drop, food for the waiting crows. The dauphin gaily suggests that they send the English food and new outfits before fighting them. Then they go forth to wipe out the enemy.

Commentary

The French contempt for their foe shows their overconfidence. At the same time, the picture of the small and ill-provided English forces will make their ultimate triumph seem the more glorious.

After Orleans calls, in the first words of the scene, "The sun doth gild our armor. Up, my lords!" he and the dauphin exchange words: "Les eaux et la terre." "L'air et le feu." They are thus summoning for support the four elements: water, earth, air and fire. The dauphin then crowns them with the heavens: "Cieux, Cousin Orleans." Now they are ready to fight.

ACT IV · SCENE 3

Summary

Henry's brothers, Gloucester and Bedford, with Exeter and Salisbury, are a little apprehensive of the outcome of the coming battle. Henry enters and, in answer to Westmoreland's sigh for another ten thousand Englishmen, he delivers the famous, superbly confident (relying on God) speech about St. Crispin's Day, in which he prophesies that Englishmen who fought at Agincourt shall be forever famed and noble. It is a masterful piece of rhetoric and has justly been a classic speech delivered before succeeding generations of the fighting English. There are in it several passages the world will not willingly let die, whether they be fighting English or not.

Westmoreland goes now to the other extreme; he would fight the battle alone with the king. The French herald enters to make a last minute offer for ransom, which Henry courteously but rather impatiently rejects in another ringing address meant, not so much for the ears of the herald, as for the ears of the Englishmen within range of his voice.

The Duke of York pleads for the privilege of leading the advance guard, or forward part of the army. Henry readily grants him the honor, the more readily as there is slight difference in position, for Henry has his troops almost in line, not in depth formation.

Commentary

The calm pride and confidence of the small band of English — the "happy few" — is contrasted with the attitude of the French leaders in the previous scene.

October 25 is the day of Saints Crispin and Crispian, humble brothers and shoemakers, who were martyred by Diocletian

at Soissons in the year 287. King Henry uses their names (which sound like *Christian*) to support the idea that God is on the side of the English. Shakespeare, however, avoids the extremely pious tone Holinshed gives Henry here. There is, in the king's final word, recognition that the result is in the hands of the Lord, but Henry does not bend to beg for victory.

Shakespeare uses the ringing sound of noble names to stir his audience, as he pictures the veterans of this battle telling of their deeds:

> Harry the king, Bedford and Exeter,
> Warwick and Talbot, Salisbury and Gloucester,
> Be in their flowing cups freshly rememb'red.

Subtle tones of irony can be found in the scene. Here Henry, by whose order Bardolph has died for stealing, says that "by the Mass" and "if God please" his soldiers will "pluck the gay new coats o'er the French soldiers' heads"(i.e., steal them).

ACT IV · SCENE 4

Summary

This comic interlude shows at least part of the battle going against the French. As he has deceived Fluellen and others by the ferocity of his manner, Pistol now manages to deceive a French gentleman of cowardly disposition. Pistol's French disintegrates completely and the boy, who has picked up a reasonable vocabulary since landing in France, has to act as interpreter, and a very good one, too. Our admiration for the boy grows gradually, and we would have liked to hear and see more of him as he developed. However, he gets Pistol the money he asks for from his dupe of a French gentleman and then tongue-lashes him to pieces. Incidentally, he provides us with news of the fate of Nym, as well as Bardolph, at which, of course, we are not surprised. Also, he forecasts his own fate in his shrewd remark that the camp and its baggage are defenceless and a French encircling movement might easily wreck it.

Commentary

The military drive of the drama continues. The battle has evidently begun, since Pistol has taken a prisoner, but the tone

lightens to a comic interlude in the way in which Pistol misunderstands and misuses the French language. Also, we are again reminded of the fate of the king's former jolly companions. We are also prepared by the boy's words about the luggage for the cowardly act of the French in Scene 7.

It may be that Pistol's triumph over the cowardly Le Fer was originally written for Falstaff. Falstaff's attitude toward honor and toward war is less humorously continued in Pistol.

An indecent tone is characteristic of Pistol's speech. He calls Le Fer a "luxurious [lustful] mountain-goat," and his play upon the Frenchman's name has obscene overtones.

Some continue to see in the deeds of the common soldiers a low echo or parody of the actions of those in power. Thus, what Pistol does with Le Fer is what Henry is doing with France.

ACT IV · SCENE 5

Summary
In another part of the field, the dauphin, the Constable of France, Orleans, Bourbon and Rambures cry out for shame at their army's defeat. The ranks are broken; all is in disorder. They resolve to stay and die.

Commentary
These twenty-three lines show how the battle is progressing. "The wretches that [they] played at dice for" have defeated the overconfident French. The French leaders, however, are not cowards.

ACT IV · SCENE 6

Summary
King Henry, on the field, meets Exeter, who tells him of the brave and piteous death of the Duke of York and the Earl of Suffolk. An alarum is heard; the scattered French are reassembling. Henry orders every soldier to kill his prisoners.

Commentary
The grimness of war is underlined, both in the loss of the two nobles and in Henry's order that the prisoners be killed.

Henry's order that the prisoners be killed, though it may sound cruel to us, was a usual precaution in the battles of those days. It was inviting to hold nobles alive for ransom, but a new attack of the "reenforced" French might give opportunity for the many prisoners to turn upon their captors.

The moving description Exeter gives of the death of York and Suffolk furthers the picture of the noble and valiant English that Shakespeare is presenting in this play. Henry's hearing the account "with mistful eyes" gives a human warmth to the leader (who in the next breath orders that all prisoners be slain). The words of the dying noble, says Stopford Brooke, "rob the battlefield of its horror and plant it with heartsease."

ACT IV · SCENE 7

Summary

Fluellen and Gower are commenting on the knavery of the French, who came behind the lines, killed the boys, and made off with the luggage, including what was in the king's tent. It is for this reason, says Gower, that "the king, most worthily, has caused every soldier to cut his prisoner's throat." Fluellen asks where "Alexander the Pig" was born. Gower corrects him: "Alexander the Great." Fluellen brushes the word aside: "The pig, or the great, or the mighty, or the huge, or the magnanimous, are all one reckoning" and compares King Henry with Alexander. One point he makes is that:

> ... As Alexander killed his friend Cleitus, being in his ales and his cups, so also Harry Monmouth, being in his right wits and his good judgments, turned away the fat knight with the great pelly doublet. He was full of jests, and gipes, and knaveries, and mocks. I have forgot his name.
> **Gow:** Sir John Falstaff.
> **Flu:** That is he. I'll tell you there is good men porn at Monmouth.
> **Gow:** Here comes his majesty.

The king bids a herald tell the French horsemen on the nearby hill to come down and fight, or leave. Otherwise, he will drive them off, and kill every man taken. Montjoy comes in,

this time not to demand ransom, but to beg for permission to count and bury the French dead. Montjoy tells Henry the English have won the day. The castle standing near the ground on which the battle was fought is called Agincourt, and Henry gives its name to the field. Fluellen reminds him of the victory over the French won by his great-uncle Edward, the Black Prince of Wales. They speak of the leek the Welsh wear in their caps upon "Saint Tavy's Day" (Saint David, the patron saint of Wales), and Fluellen declares:

> By Cheshu, I am your majesty's countryman,
> I care not who knows it, I will confess it to all
> the orld. I need not be ashamed of your majesty,
> Praised be God, so long as your majesty is an honest
> man.

"God keep me so!" says Henry, and sends his heralds with Montjoy to count the French and English dead.

The king sees the soldier, Williams, and has him brought before him questioning him about the glove in his cap. Williams tells him it's a signal for a rascal that tangled with him, whom he will strike when next they meet. He goes, and Henry gives Williams' glove to Fluellen to wear. He tells Fluellen he got it from the Duke of Alencon when they fought, and anyone challenging it is his enemy. Henry sends Fluellen to fetch Gower and then bids Warwick and Gloucester follow him to see that no harm comes between him and Williams.

Commentary

The battle over, both forces seek to care for their dead. In the moment of the king's triumph, we are reminded of his sacrifice of Falstaff. Now that the tensions of war are relaxed, the way may be prepared — with mention of the leek and Henry's giving Fluellen the glove — for lighter moments.

When Fluellen says of the fat knight, "I have forgot his name," the audience must have chuckled, for Falstaff was still a popular favorite no theatergoer would have forgotten.

Several references here may add to the irony some see beneath the surface of the story. St. David's Day may bring to mind the sinful David of the Bible, who sent Uriah to die in the forefront of a battle so that he himself might take his widow,

Bathsheba. Alexander the Great was, in the general medieval point of view, the very pattern of a great commander and a fair comparison for Henry. But Battenhouse notes that Dante puts Alexander in the circle of Hell reserved for the violent and speaks in the *Inferno* of his "blind cupidity." Henry invoked Alexander's name at Harfleur (Act III, Scene 1), and here Fluellen compares the king — observe the word that results from the Welsh mispronunciation! — with "Alexander the Pig." One may wonder if the word has a double intention.

ACT IV · SCENE 8

Summary

Williams finds Fluellen, and, recognizing his glove in Fluellen's cap, strikes him. Fluellen takes him for a traitor because Henry has told him that the glove he gave was the Duke of Alencon's. The Earl of Warwick and the Duke of Gloucester enter in time to interrupt the fight, but the king follows immediately afterward, admits his part in this foolery and has Williams' glove filled with coins and returned to him.

Henry then receives the return of dead and wounded on both sides. Here Shakespeare does follow Holinshed, but only the latter's first computation. A few words later he admits that one report is that the English lost 600. As a matter of historical fact, the loss was somewhat closer to 1,600. However, there is no doubt that the French loss was in the neighborhood of 11,000.

Henry then orders a thanksgiving Mass in the village church and afterward the resumption of the march to Calais.

Commentary

The episode of the glove is completed, to the honor of the simple English soldier. The dead are counted, thanks are given to the Lord and the victors prepare for the journey home.

Naturally, there could be no fight between the king and a common soldier. Shakespeare arranges the outcome so as to show the king generous and the soldier upright.

Henry seems particulary concerned with giving God credit for his victory, it being Elizabethan doctrine that success in arms depended, not upon strategy and strength, but upon God's favor because of the justness of one's cause. Thus, Henry's win-

ning is a proof that he is right. He several times acknowledges God as the sole source of victory: Act I, Scene 2, 289-93; Act IV, Scene 1, 306-22; and here, Act IV, Scene 8, 118-25. Perhaps he overemphasizes the thought, ordering death to any soldier who claims a share of credit for the triumph. And if the victory is due "to Thy arm alone," is God also responsible for the death of all the prisoners, whom Henry ordered slain?

ACT V · PROLOGUE

Summary

Once more, the chorus begs the audience to fill in the intervening events and scenes with their imaginations. There is nothing more vivid, compact and clear-cut by way of swift description than this prologue. The chorus describes Henry's arrival in England, his progress to Blackheath on the edge of London, his refusal to have his dinted helmet and bent sword borne ahead of him in the manner of a Roman triumph lest it be thought he was not giving the glory to God, the crowds that surged out to meet him and his final homecoming. Then, once more bridging the gap of time, he describes how the emperor, Henry's brother-in-law, came to England to try to arrange a peace — without success — and how Henry eventually returned to France.

Commentary

The audience is swept across the years between Agincourt (1415) and Henry's return to France (1420) for the Treaty of Troyes. Sigismund, head of the Holy Roman Empire, visited London in May, 1416 to seek agreement between Henry and Charles VI of France.

"The General of our gracious Empress" is another reference to the darling of the people, the Earl of Essex, who in the spring of 1599 set out with great fanfare to crush the rebellion in Ireland. The tone of the chorus' words dates the play because, by June, there were rumors that the expedition had failed and by the end of September, Essex was back from a humiliating fiasco, and in disgrace.

The lines about Julius Caesar fit the first two scenes of Shakespeare's play on Caesar, which he was probably planning at this time.

ACT V · SCENE 1

Summary

Fluellen, with a leek in his cap, comes looking for Pistol. Gower meets him and is a witness to the encounter. Fluellen does not mince matters in the names he uses, which have a strangely modern tang, but Pistol endures the insults till he is beaten. Then he begins to eat the leek as directed. When he shows signs of losing his zeal, another wallop from Fluellen gives him an added burst of speed. Gower tries to moderate Fluellen's violence, but Fluellen does not let up until Pistol has completely finished the leek and is entirely humiliated and discredited. Then Fluellen leaves abruptly.

Left alone with Gower, Pistol gives his last boast: "All hell shall stir for this." This brings down on him the most scathing and incisive dissection of his character from Gower, who leaves him utterly defeated with no future but beggary in England, because he has just heard that Pistol's wife, the hostess, is dead, and therefore, he has nowhere to retire to.

Commentary

This is the sorry end of the scabby crew of Prince Hal's former followers. The scum of London life has been brushed away. There remain the solid citizens, here represented by the Welsh Fluellen and the English Gower.

When Pistol speaks of Dame Quickly, he says "my Doll." Some editors change the name to Nell, as though Pistol (or Shakespeare) had confused Nell Quickly with Doll Tearsheet, who also died in a hospital. The word *doll*, however, was used as a general term for a woman, especially one whose moral standards were not high.

Pistol had called Fluellen a "mountain squire," a term of contempt signifying an owner of rocky, unprofitable land. Fluellen retorts that he will make Pistol a squire of low degree. The *low* is in contrast to the mountain; it also means base and it further refers to the fact that Fluellen intends to knock him down.

The place where Pistol insulted Fluellen, where he "could not breed no contention" was probably in the presence of the king, for there quarrels are forbidden. The cowardly Pistol would certainly have taken advantage of such a moment.

ACT V · SCENE 2

Summary

The French king and queen, their daughter, Katherine, the English king and their councillors meet, brought together by the Duke of Burgundy. The queen hopes that all griefs and quarrels between them will be changed to love. Burgundy pictures the disordered land of France, from which peace has gone, and hopes for its restoration. To discuss the final terms of peace, all withdraw except Katherine, her maid, Alice, and King Henry. In blunt English, Henry woos the princess. Each makes attempts at the other's language. Henry says he is a plain speaker. He hopes that she will meet him halfway, between St. Denis and St. George (the patron saints of their two countries), in the production of a son "that shall go to Constantinople and take the Turk by the beard." If she will be his, he will tell her: "England is thine, Ireland is thine, France is thine, and Henry Plantagenet is thine — who, though I speak it before his face, if he be not fellow with the best king, thou shalt find the best king of good fellows." Katherine says it will be as it shall please her father; Henry says it *shall* please him. He then wants a kiss; but Katherine protests that maidens in France do not kiss before their wedding. But when he declares "Nice customs courtesy to great kings," she permits him to embrace her.

The others return. Burgundy asks whether Henry has been teaching Katherine English. He replies that he would have her learn how perfectly he loves her. There is some light talk of blind and naked Cupid and fair French maiden cities, "all girdled with maiden walls that war hath never entered." Henry says he is content to take Kate as his wife "so the maiden cities you talk of may wait on her." All terms but one have been accepted by the French king, who now agrees to that one — namely, that in all formal documents Henry shall be addressed, in French and in Latin, as "Our Most Dear Son Henry, King of England, Heir of France."

They part on the best of terms, to prepare for the marriage and for peace.

Commentary

Henry and Katherine are brought together in this scene; peace is established; the story of Henry's triumph is at an end.

There is a double pun in the queen's remark that up to now the English eyes have borne in them "The fatal balls of murdering basilisks." The balls are both eyeballs and cannon balls, and the basilisk was both a large cannon and a fabulous serpentine monster that could kill with a look.

There is considerable word play in the wooing scene, as when Henry asks:

Hen: Do you like me, Kate?
Kath: Pardonnez-moi. I cannot tell vat is "like me."
Hen: And angel is like you, Kate, and you are like an angel.

Blundering use of the language is a sure-fire theatrical comedy device, though editors have sometimes foolishly tried to improve Katherine's English and Henry's French. There is, of course, further humor to be drawn from the need of an interpreter for their lovemaking. All of this is funnier on the stage than it may appear in print.

Within the bilingual blunders of the pair and the blunt English of Harry are suggestive undercurrents the audience might catch and some coarse references. Henry speaks of winning a lady at leapfrog, of prancing his horse for her favors; he says he will get her "with scambling."

The emphasis on the hand, discussed in the notes to Act III, Scene 4, continues in this act. Pistol plans to be a pickpocket "of quick hand." Burgundy advises Henry, in his wooing, how maids "will endure handling." And, despite his protest: "By mine honor, in true English, I love thee, Kate," it is with outstretched, grasping hand that Harry says he will marry her on the condition that the specified cities go with her into his power.

Lengthily, Henry describes himself as a plain fellow and a simple soldier. He can, however, sweep Katherine off her feet as he swept her father's soldiers off the field of Agincourt, and he no doubt considers himself a shrewd bargainer and a wise diplomat. Yet at the treaty table, he does not get the better of the French. He had earlier (end of Act II, Scene 2) sworn: "No king of England if not king of France" and had threatened to destroy all the country if it did not fully yield to him. Now he makes Katherine queen of all his lands, while he remains the "king of good fellows." From France he acquires a few

"maiden cities" and is merely named the "Heir." Shakespeare stresses this by leaving out the title "Regent," which is accorded Henry in Holinshed's account. He has not vindicated his claim by wiping out the Salic Law, which is conveniently forgotten at the treaty, but he becomes Charles' "son and heir" by marrying his daughter. He is thus, naturally, subordinate to his new "father," who remains king. In the prologue to Act III, we are told that Henry has refused the king's offer of

> Katherine his daughter, and with her, to dowry,
> Some petty and unprofitable dukedoms.

Now he is content with Katherine and some insignificant towns.

Actually, at the time of the treaty, King Charles VI was already insane, and the Duke of Burgundy acted as his regent. The dauphin stayed away.

EPILOGUE

Summary

The chorus apologizes once again for its inability to present these mighty men and great events on the little stage. This is the subject of the first quatrain of the Shakespearean sonnet in which the chorus speaks. The second quatrain reviews Henry's fortunate achievement of the crown of France, which he left to his son. The third recalls how that infant son's numerous regents mismanaged his government, resulting in the eventual loss of France. The final couplet calls attention to the three Shakespearean plays on the subject of Henry VI, with which the audience has long been familiar.

Commentary

Shakespeare places the play in its historical context. The story of the reign of the saintly innocent Henry VI was familiar to playgoers from the three parts of Shakespeare's own play about the king who lost all that his father had won. Shakespeare pays his last tribute to the ideal King Henry V, hailing him as "This star of England."

Henry V died in 1422, only two years after the treaty. Charles VI followed him in the same year. It was not the young Henry VI, however, but the dauphin, who became the next king

of France, Charles VII. Henry VI (weak, and later mad) attempted to maintain the English power in France, but his forces lost the battle of Orleans (1429) against Charles and Joan of Arc. By 1453, the only land the English had left on the Continent was Calais.

Character Sketches

Henry V

Rightly named for him, the play is dominated by Henry and would become almost a monologue if not for the members of the commonalty, who provide human or comic relief every so often and fairly regularly between serious scenes pervaded by their betters. Apart from Henry himself, Shakespeare has spent his genius entirely on them. The English nobility are minor editions of the Henry type; the French nobility are closely similar in spirit and language to the frivolous dauphin. But the minor characters are individuals of remarkable vitality, closely drawn from the life around Shakespeare or, at least, accessible to him: Mistress Quickly, Fluellen, Pistol, the boy, even Bardolph, and the three soldiers. These characters are the very life blood of drama and, since the scheme of the play is not strictly dramatic but epic, there is no real interweaving of plots. To make up for this, Shakespeare has his characters definitely divided into groups — five groups — some of which overlap while others do not, but none of them creates a real subplot of its own. The groups are Henry and the English nobility; Charles VI of France, the dauphin and the French nobility; the three rogues with their servant, the boy; the four captains in the army; and the three common soldiers.

Shakespeare has kept Henry human. In spite of his superb aspirations and noble behavior, we have a feeling that essentially he is more akin to the commonality than he is even to Westmoreland and Exeter.

Historically, Henry's reign of nine years was too short to prove that he was a great king. That he was one of the greatest generals of his time was apparent enough by the time of his death, but it must be remembered he had a much finer medium to work with than the French generals had — even if they had known how to work with it. He had a unified, dependable, independent yeomanry from England, who knew their country — squire officers trusted them and were on terms of intimacy with them — and who were known individually by those officers even up to the king himself. They were the men who did the actual fighting, and their officers fought side by side with them, or in front. The French never trusted their peasant people and hired soldiers of fortune from outside the kingdom to do the

75

dirty work. The nobility, knights and squires felt they had a monopoly on the really interesting hand-to-hand combat and preferred a scattered attack to disciplined action. The assistance of the yeomen does not detract from the credit due to Henry — the odds were terrible even with them — but, to some extent, it explains how his swift successes were possible in an age of very slow movement.

Henry did not have time to do a great deal of political consolidation in England before he set out for France. He carried on the political line by getting the nobility — always spoiling for a fight because they had not enough else to keep their minds occupied — over to France where they could do all the fighting they liked on behalf of the whole of England instead of just their own families and relatives.

After Agincourt, when Henry returned to France in 1417 with a bigger and better equipped army, the French, having learned their lesson, would not fight an open battle, but depended on a succession of fortresses which it took Henry a long time to reduce. But he did reduce them and brought France to its knees in 1420. By the Treaty of Troyes, he was named heir to the French throne, but he had not nearly enough time to consolidate his victories and, eventually, the whole of his conquests slipped through the fingers of his young son's regents.

Tall, stately and highly personable, Henry was one of the most attractive sovereigns (from the point of view of our day as well as Shakespeare's) that ever sat on the English throne. Just, human, morally upright, sympathetic to the ordinary man, he was something new in English kingship since Alfred, though there are some indications that his father's cousin, Richard II, had some of these qualities.

To Shakespeare, he seems to have been the ideal king. Edward I was perhaps another model of kingship, though he did not have the shining human sympathy which so marked Henry.

As a soldier, Henry was the first general of his time; as a stateman, he was largely untried. He was spending the profits of his father's desperate years, and he resorted to a trick — a legitimate trick — to get the unruly, anxious nobility out of the country and provide them with something to do besides cutting one another's throats.

Shakespeare telescopes judicial procedure for dramatic effect and the demands of stage presentation. Of course, the

traitor lords were actually never condemned in such a summary session as is depicted in the play. They were duly tried in the courts. But Shakespeare is following Holinshed here almost word for word, and Holinshed is either uncritical or ignorant of legal procedure. Shakespeare makes Henry wise but, above all, dramatic. He is above the torture technique of the period (one of the worst periods for that), but is a stern and relentless judge when necessary.

Of all the sovereigns of England after Alfred, Henry seems to have been better able to understand and enter into the active life, humor and sorrow of the ordinary man than any other. His personal protection of the civilian inhabitants of France from plunder is a foreshadowing of a glorious British policy and practice in Continental wars for centuries afterward. His ability to talk to, joke with and generally put himself on an equal footing with the average Englishman is, perhaps, his outstanding quality. Shakespeare might not have been willing to say so formally, but Henry acted so.

Direct and inevasive, Henry is a man of decision and action. His speech he calls plain, but it is often highly poetic. Self-control and courteous manners he has, but not without a touch of humor, sometimes mocking humor, in his remarks.

The Duke of Exeter

Right-hand advisor to Henry V, he has taken Westmoreland's place with Henry IV. As an uncle of the king and an experienced statesman and warrior (also man of business), he is entrusted by Henry with all the executive business of importance in this play.

He is left Governor of Harfleur, but he turns up at Agincourt to save the only bridge from destruction. He acts as ambassador and counsellor, as political executive and general, as warrior in hand-to-hand fighting beside the Duke of York and as statistician regarding the losses on both sides after the battle. Finally, he is head of the commissioners negotiating the Treaty of Troyes.

The Duke of York

He was a cousin of Henry IV, second cousin of Henry V and a grandson of Edward III. He was an especially favorite relative of Henry V, although he had been involved in an uprising against Henry IV.

The Earl of Westmoreland

The general executive officer to Henry IV, older now, he has yielded that place to the Duke of Exeter. Early in the play, he urges Henry on in his claims and is very decided in his appraisal of the loyalty of all Englishmen. In actual historical fact, he was not present at the Battle of Agincourt, but commanding the northern border of England against any danger of invasion from Scotland.

The Duke of Bedford

Historically, he also was not present in France at all during this campaign, for he was regent for England during Henry's absence. Dramatically, Shakespeare uses him to show Henry's close relationship with his brothers, who, after his death, played so prominent a part in the further conduct of the war.

The Duke of Gloucester

Henry V's youngest brother, although with Henry constantly throughout this play, nowhere shows himself particularly noteworthy except when in charge of the mining of the walls of Harfleur, where he does not appear personally and when, on the eve of Agincourt, he expresses the hope that the French will not attack them. For this remark, Henry reproves him and makes his reproof a half-joking series of advantages to be drawn from their dangerous situation.

The Earl of Salisbury

One of the lords attending on Henry's staff. He takes no particularly prominent part.

The Earl of Warwick

Historically, he is an example of the great lords of the period who made centralized royal rule so difficult. His son-in-law, Richard Neville, son of the Earl of Salisbury, inherited his vast holdings all over England, as well as the Salisbury estates, and was also created Earl of Warwick to keep up the succession to the title. He became the famous "King-Maker" of Henry VI's time.

The Archbishop of Canterbury

A dignified figure and an eloquent, imaginative speaker, he is clear, incisive and to the point. His lengthy discourse on the

Salic law must have bored Elizabethan audiences almost as much as it does ours. But he is a master of much more concise speech when he wants to employ it. He is astute in safeguarding the church's property by diverting the king's attention to war with a huge voluntary contribution on the part of the church. In urging the king on to the French war, he is ensuring peace at home. He is sincere in his enthusiasm for the English race and the prowess of Henry's ancestors, but his ecclesiastical interest does show through.

The Bishop of Ely

Possibly acting as Canterbury's chaplain, his role in the play is simply to break Canterbury's speeches into convenient lengths, ask the questions necessary to draw out Canterbury's replies and reinforce Canterbury's views and arguments.

The French Nobility

Charles VI

Shakespeare has strengthened the king's character somewhat in order to have an opposition to Henry that is not too unworthy. Historically, he was a very weak king who, during several periods of his life, was insane. In the play, his first appearances have a certain dignity; he grasps the significance of the danger threatening France and insists upon defensive measures being taken. However, he does not impress his court and especially his own son, the dauphin, whose attitude is insolent and insubordinate. In the last scene, he is almost a nonentity except for his rather fine speech pointing toward a peaceful and prosperous union of the two kingdoms.

The Dauphin

Shakespeare has not presented the dauphin as the warped and immoral person he really was. However, he is objectionable enough, insolent, insubordinate, opinionated and frivolous. He cannot rid himself of the obsession that Henry is a rascal of no account, the idea that prompted him to send the barrel of tennis balls. His foolish preoccupation with his armor, his horse and his mistress mark him as scarcely a serious leader. Indeed, his childish excitement and his infantile boasting over the English show the shallowness of his nature and intellect.

He disobeys his father's express command and is present at the Battle of Agincourt, but he does not appear to be seriously engaged in the fighting. However, he does attempt to rally the rear when panic and disorder have disrupted the French ranks. But then his language is feverish and extravagant. He does not talk of dying while fighting, but of committing suicide, which is a poor substitute for valor on the field.

Historically, there were three dauphins between 1415 and 1420. The one who appears in the play died shortly after the Battle of Agincourt, and his youngest brother, Charles, was dauphin by the time the Treaty of Troyes was signed.

The Constable of France

Half-brother of Charles VI, he was officially head of the French military forces. His first appearances show him head and shoulders above the king, dauphin and other French lords in character and wisdom. In the later scenes in which he appears, his character and behavior have deteriorated considerably. He is not occupied with military business, does not seem to take his duties seriously, does not inspect his position and that of the English, but relies on a report from a subordinate. He descends to the excited boasting and frivolous discussion that is the manner of the dauphin and ends the scene on the eve of battle with a foolish contest of matching proverbs with the Duke of Orleans. He makes an excited, boastful rallying speech for battle action to his fellow nobles, but his plea is far from being a match for Henry's St. Crispin's Day speech.

The Duke of Burgundy

Next to the Constable of France, he is the most imposing of the French nobility, though he would not have numbered himself among them. He was virtually an independent sovereign whose lands actually exceeded those of the king of France in extent. He is responsible for the meeting of the English and French sovereigns at Troyes and the drawing up of the peace terms. His predecessor, who has been assassinated, is named earlier in the play by Charles. The present duke is an able negotiator, and shows concern for the peace and prosperity of his people. Treating the two sovereigns as equals, he inclines to blame Charles rather than Henry for the continuance of the war but he is, undoubtedly, the master as far as Charles is concern-

ed. He is charmingly human in teasing Katherine about her coyness.

The Duke of Orleans

He is a nephew of the king of France and a cousin of the dauphin. He appears to best advantage when he stands up for the dauphin's courage when the dauphin is sneered at by the Constable of France in his absence. For the rest of his appearances in the play, he is as boastful, frivolous and contemptuous of the English as the other French lords are.

The Duke of Bretagne

His great dukedom occupies the northwest projection of France. Always a markedly independent and almost separatist section of France on account of the prevailing pure-blooded Celtic population speaking the ancient Gaelic tongue, its duke was one of the most important of the nobility. Here the duke is present twice in Act II, Scene 4, where he does not speak but receives the royal orders with the others, and in Act III, Scene 5, where he makes two speeches, both expressing his deep shame over the easy success of the English.

The Duke of Bourbon

He is named as being present only once in Act IV, Scene 5, where he tries to rally the disordered troops and throws himself back into the battle.

The Duke of Berri

He is present only in Act II, Scene 4, where he is one of the lords instructed to fortify the various towns.

Rambures

A French count, he appears in Act III, Scene 7, where he occasionally takes part in the frivolous conversation, though he makes one remark about English mastiffs that may be taken as serious. He appears also in Act IV, Scene 2, making a trivial remark about the English weeping, and in Act IV, Scene 5.

Grandpré

A count killed at Agincourt, his only appearance is in Act IV, Scene 2, where he gives a vivid description of the dejected, weary condition of the English army.

Montjoy

The royal herald of France, he does his duty courteously, frankly and impersonally. Although the words of his message are arrogant, Henry receives them as from the herald's master and compliments Montjoy on his performance, also giving him a gift. Later, when he is sent by the Constable of France, his words are too haughty and he is merely listened to. Where he appears to admit the French defeat, he is still dignified, but his attitude reveals a new humility.

Queen Isabel

Though historically she had an evil reputation, nothing of that appears in this presentation. She is gracious and queenly and pronounces a very sweet and dignified blessing on the betrothed lovers, hoping for a real union of the two kingdoms.

Katherine

She is an altogether charming girl of fourteen when she first appears, bright and eager to learn some English for she knows that fate may call her to be queen of England. In the last scene, she has developed into a gracious princess, whose beauty is famous and captures Henry's heart. Pretending to be more embarrassed than she is by Henry's direct and unconventional manner of wooing her, she leads him on with her coyness and makes no protest when he kisses her upon the lips. Historically, as in the play, she is a young lady of great fascination.

To the Shakespearean audience, she was particularly interesting as the ancestress of Queen Elizabeth for, after Henry's death and against the bitter opposition of Henry's brothers, she married Owen Tudor, a gentleman of Wales. Of course, no part of the Tudor claim to the throne could come through her.

Alice

She is the well-mannered and efficient companion of the princess, able to step in to help whenever called upon. She serves to draw out and display Katherine's character.

The Underworld Group

Bardolph

Familiar to the audience from the previous plays *Henry IV*, Part I, and *Henry IV*, Part II, his distinguishing feature is his

knobby, fiery red nose and the carbuncled red cheeks, for which he is the butt of both Falstaff's and Prince Hal's wit in the first play, and of the boy's and Fluellen's in this play. A cowardly accomplice of the highway robbery gang in the first play and an accomplice or semiservant of Falstaff's, he is made a corporal and officer's servant by the latter. In this play, he is a lieutenant, but the boy sees through him as a coward. His only show of prowess is to make enough noise to prompt Nym and Pistol to call off their quarrel and to make a half-hearted attempt to drive them to the bridge before Agincourt. His real skill is theft, and he is hanged for a trivial exercise of this, his profession.

Pistol

Already known to Shakespeare's audiences as a braggart, arrant knave and coward, Pistol has persuaded Mistress Quickly to marry him instead of Nym. He has been made an ensign (second lieutenant) in the army and given a berth in the supply department, where he hopes to be able to embezzle a fortune. Shakespeare makes him talk always in extravagant, ranting verse, with continual alliteration and inflated phrases. These tricks of speech are copied from popular plays of the day, which Shakespeare wishes to satirize. He adopts a ferocious manner and forbidding expression, which manage to impress even Fluellen and certainly Monsieur le Fer, but not the boy. Gower sees through him for the coward he is, and finally Fluellen unmasks him. Discredited, he decides to desert and adopt a life of beggary as a wounded veteran in England. Though his wife is undoubtedly in love with him, her death affects him only as a loss of quarters and provisions.

Nym

He is a corporal who is attached to the group of rogues for the first time in this play. As much a rascal as Pistol and quite as much a coward, he adopts the opposite technique to that of Pistol to cover up his cowardice. He is a man of few words, rough and to the point, together with frequent innuendoes, often meaningless. An accomplice in the thieving business, he ends up at the gallows, as Bardolph does.

The Boy

The term is the same as "garçon" in French — waiter. He is younger than the others, but still not exactly a little fellow. He

is quick of wit and intelligent. He picks up a fair command of French before he has been long in France. He is pert but only once downright impertinent, and that is when he contradicts his mistress, Dame Pistol. However, he shrewdly sees through Pistol, Bardolph and Nym and is disgusted with them. When they try to train him to pick pockets, he is outraged and resolves to leave their service, but has not managed to do so before he is cut down with all the other servants when the French raid Henry's camp at the Battle of Agincourt.

Mistress Quickly

She does not really deserve the dishonor of being called Mistress Pistol. A simple, kindly, uneducated soul, she has had an admiration for and devotion to Sir John Falstaff which has enabled the old rascal to trespass liberally upon her good nature in the matter of money, lodging, food and particularly drink. Her pathetic description of his death is a classic.

She is in love with the rascal, Pistol, and would even walk the sixteen miles to Staines with him just to bid him a longer good-bye. Her sweetness of temper is evidenced by her not taking the slightest offence at Pistol's uncalled-for advice and orders on parting. Her misuse of words and phrases is amusing, but it has its own charm.

Falstaff

Though he does not actually appear in this play, he pervades two scenes. Immensely popular with Shakespeare's audiences, he was to have appeared in this play, but Shakespeare probably came to realize that he would not fit into the atmosphere and would have to be discarded. He is perhaps the greatest comic creation in dramatic literature. Witty, humorous, clever, a born actor, he was nevertheless an old rascal who sponged on the hostess and everyone else, especially Prince Hal, and was forever swilling sherry wine. He feared no one nor any predicament and could free himself lightly and airily from any tight corner in spite of his immense size.

The Captains in the Army

Fluellen

Next to Henry, he is easily the most interesting character in the play. He is to *Henry V* what Falstaff is to *Henry IV*, Part I.

Though not nearly as neat a comic character as Falstaff, he is, at least, a more reputable one. At any rate, he furnishes most of the humor.

Always eager to talk, to argue, to show off his classical knowledge, his military knowledge, his geographical knowledge, he is opinionated, conceited, touchy and proud. That should sound like a thoroughly objectionable combination of qualities, but in Fluellen it is not so, for he combines with these so much honesty, straightforwardness, and downright good nature that he becomes a lovable character. His courage is unquestioned and witnessed by several persons. His ability as an officer is held in esteem by his superiors, though they may laugh a little at his quaint and amusing ways.

Not the least interesting thing about him is his soft Welsh accent as he speaks English. The other Welshmen in the play do not use it, but it is part of his charm, along with the quaint liberties he takes with the language, using plurals for singulars and emphasizing every point with some emphatic phrase — "see you now," "look you."

He displays obvious conceit. He insists that MacMorris has dug the mines wrongly. Later, he tells MacMorris he is as good a man as the Irishman is in every way. He talks to the king as to an equal and almost patronizes the Duke of Exeter.

His temper is Celtic, flaring quickly and quickly dying down. He has control of himself and, when struck by Williams, does not strike back because he thinks he has found a more serious matter than personal vengeance can satisfy — that is, treason. After he has justly discredited Pistol, he gives him a groat, equivalent to about fifty cents today.

His reasoning is quaint. For example, he checks Gower for talking loudly in face of an enemy who is making all kinds of noise and he compares Macedonia and Monmouth.

Provoking amusement himself, he is too serious to have a sense of humor. He takes himself very seriously. Hence, he can be jealous of MacMorris, whom the Duke of Gloucester has chosen to supervise the mining of the walls. In spite of his absurdities, he is a memorable, lovable character.

Gower
Another Welshman and a friend of Fluellen, his part in the play is to act as a foil to him and draw out his peculiarities, at

the same time moderating his excesses. He is just as learned in the classics as Fluellen and considerably more precise. Apparently, he is also as informed in all military lore.

MacMorris

He appears only once in the play, when he quarrels with Fluellen at the mention of his Irish race. Undoubtedly, he is considered capable. He has the artist's wish to try out his handiwork, the mines, now that he has them completed. He is exasperated when a parley is called and there will be no chance to use the mines. Concerning his Irish brogue, it may perhaps have been the case that the use of it was left to the individual actor, since no attempt was made to indicate it in the text.

Jamy

He loves an argument as much as Fluellen, but he also loves to listen to others dispute, whereas Fluellen could never keep out of an argument himself. There is some indication of his Scottish dialect in the text, but in this case, too, the use of it was probably left to the actor himself.

The Three Private Soldiers

Michael Williams

Apparently partly Welsh, if his name is any indication, he does not seem to have any Welsh accent. Hence, he has probably been brought up in England. He is a serious thinker and does not accept his opinions ready-made, but he admits that he really does not know the facts behind this war and is in the army only because of his duty to his king. He thinks the king may have a heavy moral responsibility for those who die in battle without their sins being confessed and forgiven. Henry convinces him that each man is the keeper of his own soul. Then Williams has the idea that the king may simply be held for ransom while the rest of them get killed. When Henry denies that this could happen, Williams tells him he is talking foolishly. When Henry reproves him, he flings out a challenge to fight, which Henry accepts. After the battle, the king plays his little practical joke on him by giving the glove to Fluellen. However, it is Williams who comes off best, for in his straightforward,

manly way, he tells the king the whole incident was his fault, and the king has to acknowledge this. Williams will accept the coins from Henry because he is the king, but he will accept no gifts from one who is not far from his own social station.

John Bates

Worried over the precarious situation at Agincourt, he is quite ready to do his duty in the coming battle. He does not seek to know the rights and wrongs of the king's cause. It is sufficient for him that his duty is to fight for the king. If the king's cause is wrong, his duty to the king will absolve him from blame.

Alexander Court

He speaks only to notice the first streaks of dawn as he thinks. For the rest of his brief appearance in the play, he merely listens.

Classical Allusions

Agamemnon: The leader of the Greeks against Troy. According to Homer he was pre-eminent among the Greeks for dignity, power and majesty. "He is the *'king of men.'*" "The Duke of Exeter is as magnanimous as *Agamemmon*" (Act III, Scene 6), says Fluellen of the duke, when he is describing the passage of arms at the bridge.

Alexander: Alexander the Great, son of Philip, King of Macedon. His conquests over the Persians and in Asia Minor gained for him the name of *Great*. There are the following allusions to him in the play:

"The Gordian knot" (Act I, Scene 1, 46). (See Gordias.)

"Fathers that, like so many *Alexanders*" (Act III, Scene 1, 19), alluding to the victories gained by the English over the French. The great battles of Cressy and Poitiers, in which large numbers of the French were defeated by a comparative handful of Englishmen, might well be compared with the triumphs of the disciplined Greeks over the Persian hordes.

"His father was called Philip of Macedon" (Act IV, Scene 7, 17). From this information transmitted to him by Gower, Fluellen deduces a comparison between Macedon and Monmouth.

"Did in his ales and his angers, look you, kill his pest friend, Cleitus" (Act IV, Scene 7, 34). (See Cleitus.)

From this, Fluellen deduces a comparison between Alexander and Henry V. The former, in a fit of intoxication, killed his friend Cleitus; the latter, in sober judgment, committed Falstaff to prison and broke the knight's heart.

Barbason: "I am not *Barbason,* you cannot conjure me" (Act II, Scene 1, 47). The name is that of a fiend. The name also occurs in the *Merry Wives of Windsor*.

Bartholomew-tide: "Like flies at *Bartholomew-tide*"(Act V, Scene 2, 292). August 24th, which day has been assigned for the commemoration of the apostle, Bartholomew.

Brutus:

> Were but the outside of the *Roman Brutus*
> Covering discretion with a coat of folly (Act II,
> Scene 4, 37-8).

Lucius Junius Brutus, the great hero of the Roman legends connected with the expulsion of the Tarquins, was nephew of King Tarquinius Superbus. His elder brother was murdered by Tarquinius, and Lucius escaped his brother's fate by feigning stupidity, which is how he received the name of Brutus. The manner in which he revealed his real nature and caused the Romans to expel the Tarquins after Lucretia had stabbed herself is a well-known story in Roman history. Upon the expulsion of the Tarquins he was elected one of the first consuls.

As Brutus feigned stupidity to save his life, while really he was a man of great ability, so Henry V had in his youth concealed his many good parts under the guise of the reckless behavior of a wild youth.

Cadwallader: The last of the Welsh or British Kings. He lived in the middle of the seventh century. He bravely defended Wales against the attacks of the Saxons. He received the name of "Blessed." Another account represents him as having been compelled to leave Britain because of pestilence and famine. He went first to America and then to Rome, where he was baptized and received the name of Peter.

"Not for *Cadwallader* and all his goats" (Act V, Scene 1, 25). In this oath, Pistol contemptuously refers to Welshmen, whose chief wealth lay in goats fed on the scanty mountain pastures.

Cleitus or Clitus: "Alexander killed his friend *Cleitus* being in his ales and his cups" (Act IV, Scene 7, 40). An intimate friend of Alexander the Great and one of his generals, he saved Alexander's life at the battle of the Granicus. Some six or seven years later, he was slain by Alexander at a banquet. Both king and general had partaken freely of wine, and Cleitus had roused the king's anger by his insolent language. Alexander felt bitter remorse for the death of his friend.

Cressida: "Fetch forth the lazar kite of Cressid's kind" (Act II, Scene 1, 73). A beautiful woman, her name is associated with infidelity. She was the daughter of Calchas, the Grecian priest, and went to the siege of Troy. Being captured by the Trojans, she betrothed herself to Troilus, one of the sons of Priam. The lovers vowed eternal fidelity and, as pledges, Troilus gave Cressida a sleeve, while she gave him a glove. Soon afterward, an exchange of prisoners was made. Cressida vowed to remain constant to Troilus, but soon transferred her affection to Diomede. She even gave him the glove of Troilus to wear.

Crispin Crispian: "And *Crispin Crispian* shall ne'er go by" (Act IV, Scene 3, 57). The allusion is to the saints, Chrispinus and Chrispianus, two brothers, who were shoemakers. They were born in Italy, but journeyed to Soissons, France (about A.D. 303) in order to preach the Gospel. They worked at their trade in order to support themselves. They suffered martyrdom October 25th of the year they entered Soissons and were regarded as the patron saints of shoemakers. The Battle of Agincourt was fought on October 25th, the anniversary of the martyrdom of the two brothers. Henry alludes to the day under both names.

Elysium: That part of the realms of the dead which was the residence of the spirits of the blessed and where they enjoyed perfect happiness. King Henry, in contrasting the monarch with the peasant, admits that the latter toils hard during the day, but "all night sleeps in *Elysium*" (Act IV, Scene 1, 262) — that is, enjoys unbroken sleep.

Fortune, the goddess of fortune: She was represented as having different attributes:

    (1)   with a rudder, as guiding and conducting the affairs of the world.

    (2)   with a wheel, *"Giddy Fortune's fickle wheel"* (Act III, Scene 6, 24), which Fluellen construes *"to signify to you, which is the moral of it, that she is turning, and inconstant, and unstability, and variation"* (Act III, Scene 6, 33).

(3)   with a ball, as representing the varying unsteadiness of fortune. *"She stands upon the rolling restless stone,"* says Pistol, and Fluellen explains *"her foot, look you, is fixed upon a spherical stone which rolls and rolls and rolls."*

(4)   as blind, representing the blind chance displayed in the bestowal of her favors. *"That goddess blind,"* says Pistol, and Fluellen explains *"Fortune is painted plind with a muffler afore her eyes, to signify to you that Fortune is blind."*

Gordias: "The *Gordian knot* of it he will unloose"(Act I, Scene 1, 46). Gordias was a Phrygian peasant, chosen by the Phrygians as their king. In gratitude, he dedicated his wagon to Jupiter and tied the pole to the yoke with a rope of bark so artfully that the ends of the cord could not be discovered. An oracle declared that he who untied this knot would be king of Asia. When Alexander the Great was shown the knot, he cut it with his sword, saying, "It is thus we loose our knots."

"To cut the Gordian knot" has become proverbial for the solution of a difficult problem. The Archbishop of Canterbury describes King Henry's ingenuity as being able to solve any difficult political question with ease.

The Hydra: "Nor never *Hydra-headed* wilfulness" (Act I, Scene 1, 35). The Lernean Hydra. It was one of the labors of Hercules to destroy this monster, which ravaged the country of Lernea. In appearance like a lion, it had nine heads, of which the middle one was immortal. As fast as Hercules struck off one of the heads with his club, two new ones sprang up in its place. The hero accomplished his task by burning away the heads and by burying the ninth or immortal one under a rock.

Hyperion: Helios or Sol, the god of the sun, was the son of Hyperion, and thus is often called by the patronymic *Hyperion* (short for *Hyperionion*). He was supposed to drive the sun in its course in the heavens in a chariot drawn by horses. "Doth rise and help *Hyperion* to his horse" (Act IV, Scene 1, 263). This describes the early rising of the

laborer who, up before sunrise, is metaphorically supposed to assist Hyperion in harnessing his steeds to his chariot.

Jove: "In thunder and in earthquake like a *Jove*" (Act II, Scene 4, 100). Jove or Jupiter was the king of the gods. He was lord of heaven and thus was worshipped as the god of rain, storms, thunder and lightning. King Henry, in his invasion of France, is described as descending upon the land in a tempest of lightning and earthquake.

Macedon: "Alexander the Great was born in *Macedon*" (Act IV, Scene 7, 18). A country north of Greece rendered famous in ancient history (1) by Philip of Macedonia, who organized his army on the plan of the phalanx and established Macedonia as mistress of Greece and as a powerful military state; (2) by Alexander the Great, who led the Macedonians into Asia, defeated the Persians and founded the great Macedonian Empire. The Macedonian kings exercised sovereignty over Greece till the conquest of Perseus by the Romans (B.C. 168). Macedon was a district, but Fluellen speaks of it as if it were a town.

Mark Antony: The well-known Marcus Antonius, the friend of Caesar, and one of the first triumvirate, Antony, Octavius and Lepidus. He had the reputation of being a brave and skilful general. Fluellen, before he discovered Pistol's real character, thought him "as valiant a man as *Mark Antony*" (Act III, Scene 7, 13).

Mars: "Assume the port of *Mars*" (Act I, Prologue, 6). The Roman god of war. In the first Prologue, the chorus desires poetic fire to describe adequately King Henry. Then (such was that king's renown in war), he would appear in carriage and bearing a veritable Mars — *a god of war*.

"Big *Mars* seems bankrupt in their beggar'd host" (Act IV, Scene 2, 43). A description in the mouth of Grandpré of the English host before the Battle of Agincourt. Such is their sorry appearance — rusty armor, war-worn, mean, and tired horses — that all spirit of battle seems to be lacking in them.

Mercury: "With winged heels as English *Mercuries*" (Act II, Prologue, 7). The Roman god, Mercurius, corresponding to the Greek god, Hermes. The herald of gods, and as such regarded as the god of eloquence. The principal attributes of Hermes are: (1) A travelling hat with a broad brim; (2) the herald's staff; (3) the golden sandals, provided with wings at the ankles, which carried the god across land and sea with the rapidity of the wind. The allusion is to the English hosts assembling with marvellous speed at the summons of their king and crossing the English Channel with surprising quickness.

Hermes is said to have invented both the lyre and the syrinx, or the shepherd's pipe. The dauphin says that the basest horn of his charger's hoof "is more musical than the pipe of *Hermes*" (Act III, Scene 7, 17).

Muse: The Muses were nine in number; the following are their names and symbols:

Calliope, the epic muse: a tablet and stylus, sometimes a scroll.

Clio, muse of history: a scroll, or open chest of books.

Erato, muse of love ditties: a lyre.

Euterpe, muse of lyric poetry: a flute.

Melpomene, muse of tragedy: a tragic mask, the club of Hercules, or a sword.

Polyhymnia, muse of sacred poetry: sits pensive, but has no symbol.

Terpsichore, muse of choral song and dance: a lyre and the plectrum.

Thalia, muse of comedy and idyllic poetry: a comic mask, a shepherd's staff, or a wreath of ivy.

Urania, muse of astronomy: carries a staff pointing to a globe.

The Muses were, according to the earliest writers, the inspiring goddesses of song. Later, they were regarded as the divinities presiding over the different kinds of poetry and over the arts and sciences.

O for a *muse of fire,* that would ascend
The brightest heaven of invention (Act I, Prologue).

The allusion clearly has reference to the early notion of an "inspiring goddess," though some commentators think otherwise. Warburton sees a reference to "the Peripatetic system which imagines several heavens one above another, the last and highest of which was one of fire." Johnson thinks there is a reference "to the aspiring nature of fire, which by its levity, at the separation of the chaos, took the highest seat of all the elements." But Douce explains that Shakespeare "simply wishes for poetic fire and a due proportion of inventive genius."

Parcae: The Fates, who spin the thread of human life. According to Hesiod, they were three in number: *Clotho* (represented with a spindle), who spun the thread; *Lachesis*, who drew it out; and *Atropos,* who cut it or broke it off. "Dost thou thirst, base Trojan, to have me fold up *Parca's* fatal web" (Act V, Scene 1, 18). Thus, Pistol pompously addresses Fluellen, threatening his life in elevated language. Fluellen responds by making him eat the leek.

Pegasus: The famous winged horse, by whose aid Bellerophon overcame the Chimaera. The dauphin compares his horse to Pegasus, calling it "le cheval, volant, the *Pegasus*"—that is, the flying horse, Pegasus (Act III, Scene 7, 14). Pegasus is said to have come into existence when Perseus struck off the head of the Gorgon Medusa (see Perseus).

Perseus: He is mentioned with reference to the flying horse, Pegasus. The dauphin speaks of his horse as "le cheval, volant, the Pegasus," and styles it "a beast for *Perseus*" (Act III, Scene 7, 11). Perseus, as the story goes, was sent to fetch the head of the Gorgon Medusa. He succeeded, and from the dead Medusa sprang the winged horse, Pegasus. It would appear that Shakespeare regards Pegasus as the horse of Perseus, which was not the case. Bellerophon was the only mortal who seems to have ridden the flying horse.

Phoebus: "With silken streamers the young *Phoebus* fanning" (Act III, Prologue, 6). The god of the sun; young Phoebus

is a reference to the early sun, or early morning.

"Sweats in the eye of *Phoebus*" (Act IV, Scene 1, 261) refers to the toils of the laborer, working in the heat of the day.

Pompey: "But to examine the wars of *Pompey the Great,* you shall find, I warrant you, that there is no tiddle taddle, nor pibble pabble in *Pompey's camp*" (Act IV, Scene 1, 69-70). Fluellen desires that the English soldiers should keep silence when near the enemies' camp. He mentions Pompey as a great master of the art of war, in whose camp the strictest discipline would be kept.

Pompey first displayed his great military abilities as one of Sulla's generals in the Marian war. On his return from this war, he was greeted by Sulla with the title of Magnus (Great), a title which he retained ever afterward and handed down to his children.

St. David: "I'll knock his leek about his pate upon *Saint David's Day* " (Act IV, Scene 1, 55). He is the uncle of King Arthur. He first embraced monastic life in the Isle of Wight and subsequently removed to Menevia, in Pembrokeshire, where he founded twelve convents. When he became archbishop, he removed the See from Carleon to Menevia, which was subsequently called St. David's, and became the metropolis of Wales. He died in 642 A.D. *St. David's Day* is March 1st, when Welshmen wear a leek in commemoration of a great victory over the Saxons (640 A.D.). The victory is ascribed "to the prayers of St. David," and to his suggestion that the Welshmen (or Britons) should wear a leek in their cap so that they might readily recognize each other. It is said that the Saxons, having no badge, frequently attacked their own men.

St. Denis: "St. Denis be my speed" (Act V, Scene 2, 178). The patron saint of France; his day is October 9th.

Saint George: "Cry 'God for Harry, England and *Saint George,*' " (Act III, Scene 1, 34). The patron saint of England, adopted as such in consequence of the miraculous assistance rendered by him to the arms of the Christians under Godfrey de Bouillon during the first crusade.

Tartarus: "He might return to vasty *Tartar* back" (Act II, Scene 2, 123). The lower world, situated below Hades, this is the hell of torment of the ancients, where the spirits of wicked men are punished.

Points of Interest

Anachronisms

An anachronism is the assigning by an author of an event or a practice or an instrument to a date to which it cannot belong.

1. "Pistol's cock is up." Act II, Scene 1, 55. The weapon was not invented till 1545 in Florence, Italy.
2. "Art thou Bedlam?" Act V, Scene 1, 20. Bedlam is a contraction of the word Bethlehem, the name of a religious establishment in London, suppressed with the rest of the monasteries in Henry VIII's reign in 1533. It was then converted into a madhouse.
3. "That shall go to Constantinople and take the Turk by the beard?" The Turks did not capture Constantinople until 1453, and Henry is represented as saying this in 1420.
4. "'Tis a goot silling." Act IV, Scene 8, 62. The shilling was first coined about 1502, in the reign of Henry VII.

Historical Inaccuracies

1. Westmoreland was not at Agincourt; he was in charge of defences on the Scottish border.
2. Bedford was not at Agincourt; he was regent in England.
3. Warwick was not at Agincourt; he was Governor of Calais at the time.
4. The Duke of Exeter was not created duke until a year after Agincourt, 1446. He was the Earl of Dorset at the time of this play.
5. The dauphin was not present at Agincourt.
6. Shakespeare makes no distinction between the Duke of Burgundy, who was murdered in 1419 and had been mentioned earlier in the play, and his successor, who negotiated for the Treaty of Troyes.

Henry's Claim to the French Throne

Henry V based his claim to the throne of France on the right and claim of his great-grandfather, Edward III. Edward III based his claim on the rights of his mother, Isabella of France, daughter of Philip IV and wife of Edward II of England. But, granting that the raising of the point of this Salic

law was a mere quibble on the part of the French, Charles of Navarre had a better right than Edward III of England through his mother, Jane of Navarre, daughter of Philip IV's eldest son.

Besides, Edward III, by the Treaty of Bretigny in 1360, expressly renounced any claim of the sovereigns of England to the throne of France.

In other words, Henry V had no claim whatever.

Conviction of the Conspirators

In the play, it would seem that the conspirators are executed without trial. Of course, this did not happen. The Earl of Cambridge and Sir Thomas Grey were tried before a county jury of twelve men and found guilty of treason in conspiring to proclaim Edmund Mortimer, Earl of March, king and calling in a Scottish army. Lord Scroop was also tried before the county jury and found guilty of misprision (concealment) of treason. Grey was forthwith beheaded. The Earl of Cambridge and Lord Scroop claimed the right of being tried by their peers. They were granted the right, and a court was constituted consisting of all the lords in Henry's army, who unanimously convicted them.

Interestingly enough, it was that very Edmund Mortimer, Earl of March, on whose behalf the conspirators were scheming, who tipped the king off concerning the plot. He was a close friend of Henry.

Dramatic Irony

This term applies to a situation in which the audience has information which the characters, or one set of the characters on the stage, does not possess. It can also refer to a circumstance in which one set of characters on the stage has information that another set has not.

Instances: Act II, Scene 2. Henry causes the conspirators to sentence themselves. Then he gives them their commissions, as they suppose, but he alone knows that they are indictments.

Act III, Scene 7. The whole scene is an example of dramatic irony, for the audience knows what is going to happen to these boastful, disdainful French lords.

Two Main Issues in *Henry V*

Henry V builds its story around two problems that concerned the Elizabethans. The first of these is the problem of

kingship: what are the privileges and responsibilities of a king and what sort of king should there be to exercise them? Rowse remarks that (as a lingering habit from the playwright's schoolday training in rhetoric) many of Shakespeare's plays have one long set speech on a theme closely related to the essence of the play. In *King John* it is commodity (expediency); in *As You Like It* it is the Seven Ages of Man; in *Henry V* it is ceremony. The king, after all, "is but a man," except for the golden barriers of court procedure that distinguish his behavior. Henry's French opponent and his own son are both so human — all too human — that they go mad.

More pervasive is the problem of war, which, of course, is linked with the question of the king's responsibility to and for his subjects. The horrors of war are several times detailed through the mouth of Henry, yet it was he that initiated the war for his personal ambitions. The virtues and vices of war are weighed in the play. On the one hand is the king's self-control and his reliance on God to give the victory to the righteous; in all ranks of the army there is patriotism, bravery, devotion. On the other hand is corruption and brutality; the tricky arguments of the professional soldier; the heroics of war disgraced in the characters of Pistol and his crew; cowardice and opportunism. It may be brought to mind that at the siege of Rouen, a year after Agincourt and before the treaty that ends the play, the city expelled some twelve thousand women, children and old men, who would have weakened its defence. Since Henry would not permit them to pass through his lines, they died of starvation.

The French

The treatment of the French in the play should be noted. They are overconfident in talk, but the long roll of dead nobles shows that they were courageous in battle. Henry despises the dauphin, but the king (Charles VI) — even though, historically, he was already insane — is shown as a dignified ruler. Perhaps this is because he was Katherine's father. After Henry's death in 1422, his widow, Katherine, married Owen Tudor and was grandmother of Henry VII, first of the Tudor kings, whose line continued in Elizabeth. The Elizabethans, in any event, took the French seriously, as formidable adversaries.

Against the French, Henry's son was powerless, and the epilogue — most unusually, but with an eye to the Elizabethans'

knowledge of the story — reminds us of the later crumbling of all that Henry V had gained abroad. Also in this play, under the bright fanfare and gilt costumes of patriotism and power, Shakespeare lets peep the soiled garments of violence and greed.

Critical Appraisal

As a consequence of the emphasis on the play's epic flow rather than the dramatic drive in *Henry V*, five different judgments of *Henry V* may be traced among the critical discussions.

1) It is a bad play. Henry is a man of action, but has little to do that is dramatically interesting. The play is a dramatic failure, appealing to a "puerile patriotism" with a king who resembles "a hearty undergraduate." Henry breaks through the heavy line for the winning touchdown. Such writers as Hazlitt, Yeats, Mark Van Doren and Masefield share this opinion, some stressing the frequency of animal imagery in the play, even remarking on Henry's wishing he could marry Katherine as nimbly as he vaults onto a horse.

2) It is an excellent play. For every ten that are disappointed in *Henry V*, a thousand rally to its call. It is "the peak of the history plays," winning response in every patriotic heart. Stopford Brooke is representative of this opinion: "All that makes the heart of England great is tried to the uttermost. It was the noble soul of England that conquered at Agincourt." Ruskin called the Agincourt episode "one of the most perfect things, in its sort, we have anywhere of Shakespeare's." J. Dover Wilson and J.H. Walter in the introductions, respectively, of the New Cambridge and the New Arden editions of the play, join in this praise. It may, indeed, be argued with some justification that, if we see in Henry less than the pattern of an ideal king, it is because our criteria of kingship have changed.

Not content with either of these judgments, recent critics have sought to probe further.

3) Some declare that Shakespeare, in his objective portrait, could not help letting the shoddier reality show beneath the glamor and the splendor of the ideal king. Ruthlessness and splendor are inseparable aspects of war, and as the warrior Henry moves toward his triumph, the man Henry loses his warm-heartedness. He seeks to make contact with his soldiers, but they do not recognize their heroic leader disguised in a captain's cloak, and his treatment of Williams is political rather than human. He may be loved by many, but he gives no sign of loving anyone. Nor does he give any indication that he recognizes his former companions, whom he abandons to their shabby ends. John Palmer puts the contrast well:

Henry's heroic speeches are, of their kind, the best ever trumpeted by a martial poet from the battlements of time. But the human interest of the play lies elsewhere. It is to be sought in the constant effort of the shrinking man to come to terms with the swelling monarch.

4) Other critics declare that the playwright deliberately fashioned this ironic contrast between the diamond appearance and the coal-dust fact. Some feel that there is an inevitable conflict between the ideal conception of high office and the practical deals and compromises necessary to maintain it. In his dealings with his own high clergy and his claim to the French crown, Henry, says Goddard, made himself into "something that comes too close for comfort to Machiavelli's ideal prince." And Shakespeare's representation of this, adds Stopford Brooke, "is a masterpiece of sugared scorn and indignation." The indignation, you notice, is felt, not by the king nor by the clergy, but by Shakespeare. Thus, while the chorus continues the glorification of the patriot king, Shakespeare — in this view — makes sure to expose the wicked futility of his enterprise and the callous reasoning of the man.

5) A final few hold still another opinion. They contend that Shakespeare had little regard for Henry, but a deep love for England, and that the personality of the king is submerged in the tribute to the spirit and the glory of the land. The play's original purpose, they suggest, is lost in the power of the heroic drive.

Whichever of these five opinions of the play a critic may hold, it is interesting to observe that all critics speak of Henry as a real, living person. He is not a character in a drama, but a historical figure shown in action.

Selected Criticisms

This play has many scenes of high dignity, and many of easy merriment. The character of the King is well supported, except in his courtship, where he has neither the vivacity of *Hal*, nor the grandeur of *Henry*. The humour of *Pistol* is very happily continued; his character has perhaps been the model of all the bullies that have yet appeared on the *English* stage.

The lines given to the chorus have many admirers; but the truth is, that in them a little may be praised, and much must be forgiven; nor can it be easily discovered why the intelligence given by the chorus is more necessary in this play than in many others where it is omitted. The great defect of this play is the emptiness and narrowness of the last act, which a very little diligence might have easily avoided.

Samuel Johnson, Johnson on Shakespeare, 1908.

. . . I have often had the fancy that there is some one myth for every man, which, if we but knew it, would make us understand all he did and thought. Shakespeare's myth, it may be, describes a wise man who was blind from very wisdom, and an empty man who thrust him from his place, and saw all that could be seen from very emptiness. It is in the story of Hamlet, who saw too great issues everywhere to play the trivial game of life, and of Fortinbras, who came from fighting battles about 'a little patch of ground' so poor that one of his captains would not give 'six ducats' to 'farm it,' and who was yet acclaimed by Hamlet and by all as the only befitting king. And it is in the story of Richard II, that unripened Hamlet, and of Henry V, that ripened Fortinbras. To pose character against character was an element in Shakespeare's art, and scarcely a play is lacking in characters that are the complement of one another, and so, having made the vessel of porcelain, Richard II, he had to make the vessel of clay, Henry V. He makes him the reverse of all that Richard was. He has the gross vices, the coarse nerves, of one who is to rule among violent people, and he is so little 'too friendly' to his friends that he bundles them out of doors when their time is over. He is as remorseless and undistinguished as some natural force, and the finest thing in his play is the way his old companions fall out of it broken-hearted or on their way to the gallows; and instead of that lyricism which rose

103

out of Richard's mind like the jet of a fountain to fall again where it had risen, instead of that fantasy too enfolded in its own sincerity to make any thought the hour had need of, Shakespeare has given him a resounding rhetoric that moves men as a leading article does to-day. His purposes are so intelligible to everybody that everybody talks of him as if he succeeded, although he fails in the end, as all men great and little fail in Shakespeare. His conquests abroad are made nothing by a woman turned warrior. That boy he and Katharine were to 'compound,' 'half French, half English,' 'that' was to 'go to Constantinople and take the Turk by the beard,' turns out a saint and loses all his father had built up at home and his own life.

Shakespeare watched Henry V not indeed as he watched the greater souls in the visionary procession, but cheerfully, as one watches some handsome spirited horse, and he spoke his tale, as he spoke all tales, with tragic irony.

William Butler Yeats, *Essays and Introductions*, 1961.

. . . To come, then, to Henry. Both as prince and as king he is deservedly a favourite, and particulary so with English readers, being, as he is, perhaps the most distinctively English of all Shakespeare's men. In *Henry V,* he is treated as a national hero. In this play he has lost much of the wit which in him seems to have depended on contact with Falstaff, but he has also laid aside the most serious faults of his youth. He inspires in a high degree fear, enthusiasm, and affection; thanks to his beautiful modesty he has the charm which is lacking to another mighty warrior, Coriolanus; his youthful escapades have given him an understanding of simple folk, and sympathy with them; he is the author of the saying, 'There is some soul of goodness in things evil'; and he is much more obviously religious than most of Shakespeare's heroes. Having these and other fine qualities, and being without certain dangerous tendencies which mark the tragic heroes, he is, perhaps, the most *efficient* character drawn by Shakespeare, unless Ulysses, in *Troilus and Cressida,* is his equal. And so he has been described as Shakespeare's ideal man of action; nay, it has even been declared that here for once Shakespeare plainly disclosed his own ethical creed, and showed us his ideal, not simply of a man of action, but of a man.

But Henry is neither of these. The poet who drew Hamlet and Othello can never have thought that even the ideal man of action would lack that light upon the brow which at once transfigures them and marks their doom. It is as easy to believe that, because the lunatic, the lover, and the poet are not far apart, Shakespeare would have chosen never to have loved and sung. Even poor Timon, the most inefficient of the tragic heroes, has something in him that Henry never shows. Nor is it merely that his nature is limited: if we follow Shakespeare and look closely at Henry, we shall discover with the many fine traits a few less pleasing. Henry IV. describes him as the noble image of his own youth; and, for all his superiority to his father, he is still his father's son, the son of the man whom Hotspur called a 'vile politician.' Henry's religion, for example, is genuine, it is rooted in his modesty; but it is also superstitious — an attempt to buy off supernatural vengeance for Richard's blood; and it is also in part political, like his father's projected crusade. Just as he went to war chiefly because, as his father told him, it was the way to keep factious nobles quiet and unite the nation, so when he adjures the Archbishop to satisfy him as to his right to the French throne, he knows very well that the Archbishop *wants* the war, because it will defer and perhaps prevent what he considers the spoliation of the Church. This same strain of policy is what Shakespeare marks in the first soliloquy in *Henry IV.*, where the prince describes his riotous life as a mere scheme to win him glory later. It implies that readiness to use other people as means to his own ends which is a conspicuous feature in his father; and it reminds us of his father's plan of keeping himself out of the people's sight while Richard was making himself cheap by his incessant public appearances. And if I am not mistaken there is a further likeness. Henry is kindly and pleasant to every one as Prince, to every one deserving as King; and he is so not merely out of policy: but there is no sign in him of a strong affection for any one, such an affection as we recognise at a glance in Hamlet and Horatio, Brutus and Cassius, and many more.

We do not find this in *Henry V.*, not even in the noble address to Lord Scroop, and in *Henry IV,* we find, I think, a liking for Falstaff and Poins, but no more: there is no more than a liking, for instance, in his soliloquy over the supposed corpse of his fat friend, and he never speaks of Falstaff to Poins with any

affection. The truth is, that the members of the family of Henry IV. have love for one another, but they cannot spare love for any one outside their family, which stands firmly united, defending its royal position against attack and instinctively isolating itself from outside influence.

A.C. Bradley, "The Rejection of Falstaff," *Oxford Lectures on Poetry*, 1909.

In popular estimation Shakespeare's Henry V is probably a more perfect king than Henry IV. Admittedly he is a far more likeable fellow — once he has ceased to explain his wild oats. And what enterprises of kingship he undertakes he performs no less successfully than did his father. But Shakespeare can only allow him to purchase our personal affection by considerably reducing his duties as a king. His father had to exercise the whole art of government, maintaining peace at home and securing glory abroad. It was in the more exacting office of governing at home that his subtlest craft was needed. But Hal is largely relieved of these routine trials, and for the most part his kingship is circumscribed to military leadership. At the head of his army, in embarkation, in siege, and in battle, he treads the surest of traditional ways to popular acclamation. He is a great commander whose greatness as a king is tacitly and sentimentally assumed. In a field-command he can keep so much of the humanity he would perforce have to leave outside the door of civil office. Soldiers are much more obviously human than clerks of the Treasury.

But on the rare occasions when Hal is called upon for a definitely political decision, are the factors determining political wisdom different from what they were in his father's case? Hal's mode of leading his army to victory is his most obvious national asset. But it was, so to speak, a secondary achievement, and the good it did was entirely dependent on the prior decision to make war on France. The first scene of *Henry V* — a scene which critics curiously pass by — unmistakably deprives Hal of all personal credit for that decision. He is trapped into declaration of war by the machinations of a group of men whose sole and quite explicit motive is to preserve their own revenues; and the political implication is more flagrant in that these men are an ecclesiastical synod. Hal, in fact, owes his political achievement, not as did his father, to his own insight, but rather to

something so near to intellectual dullness that it permits of his being jockeyed into his opportunities. . . .

To a large extent, Henry V is thrust into political greatness by sheer instinct. His genius leads him to take steps his moral nature would have prohibited his taking; and his ingratiating commonplaceness of mind hides from him their immoral implications or even glosses them with conventional moral sanction. He is secured in our affections, because he is dispensed by Shakespeare from requiring such intellectual greatness as his father had . . . . Henry V wins our hearts as the greatest of plain men. His common text is that the king is but a man; that all his senses have but human conditions, and that, his ceremonies laid by, in his nakedness he appears but a man. Note, however, how his guardian angel saw to it that he should preserve his incognito whilst preaching this sermon. Henry has all the admirable propensities of the average Englishman, his conventions, his manners, and his opportune lack of them, his prejudices, and even his faith . . . . In all except generalship, he is that most attractive and delightful being, the magnificent commonplace, and we needs must love the glorified image of ourselves.

Thus did Shakespeare sweeten the savour of the political life, without giving the lie to what he had apprehended of its sordid necessities. Though it may be largely hidden, the truth, as Shakespeare grasped it, remains even in *Henry V:* the sense that not only is politics a nasty business, but that a repugnant unscrupulousness is an invaluable asset in the art of government. That is the burden of the English History Plays, jubilant as they are in pride of country and of race.

H.B. Charlton, *Shakespeare, Politics, and Politicians, 1929.*

Was Henry, then, as some have thought, Shakespeare's ideal? Gervinus and other German critics have declared he was, being the antithesis of Richard II and Hamlet. Some of them have even gone so far as to say that Henry is Shakespeare himself, with his practical genius and well-balanced nature, his taste for the low as well as the lofty, and his sense of humor in the midst of duty — his liking for play when at work. Mr. W. B. Yeats holds just the contrary. Poet of the Celtic twilight, of them that went forth to battle but always fell, he thinks that Shakespeare infinitely preferred Richard; and that Henry is given the "gross vices and coarse nerves," and " the resounding

rhetoric, as of a leading article,'' which befit a man who succeeds, though his success was really failure. "Shakespeare watched Henry V, not indeed as he watched the greater souls in the visionary procession, but cheerfully, as one watches some handsome spirited horse, and he spoke his tale, as he spoke all tales, with tragic irony.'' But when Shakespeare — when any popular dramatist — is ironical, we the people must needs know it; or else his popular art has failed him and missed the mark. Here is no evidence of either. Instead of being sly, or insinuating, or pregnant of innuendo, he is more exuberant and enthusiastic than usual; the choruses, which are the authentic voice of the poet himself, put that beyond the peradventure of a doubt. And the likelihood is that Professor Dowden is nearer the truth; Henry V, at least in some measure, approaches Shakespeare's ideal of the practical man, which is not his highest ideal. Shakespeare, no doubt, admired success, though without worshipping it; he himself succeeded, not inconsiderably in his brief two score and ten; but the men he admired most, I daresay, were the finer spirits such as Hamlet, Brutus, or Prospero, whether they succeeded or failed. It was their devotion and gallantry that he admired, not (pessimistically or sentimentally) their devotion and gallantry foiled or thrown away.

It is more to the point to say that Henry is the ideal of England, not Shakespeare's but his country's notion of their hero-king. He is the king that audiences at the Globe would have him be. This is particularly true as regards what we nowadays consider his bragging, his priggishness and cant. The obtrusive morality and piety were expected; for that matter they are like the sort of thing you find in a Speech from the Throne or our American Presidential Thanksgiving proclamations at the present day. Officially, piety has been ever in favor; even in ungodly America ceremonies so diverse as the laying of a corner stone and the conferring of the German degree of Ph.D. are performed in the name of the Father, the Son, and the Holy Ghost; and in the new Assembly of Southern Ireland, I notice, the order is given by the Speaker to "call the roll in the name of God.''

And on the Elizabethan stage piety and morality are as inseparable from the ideal king as the crown on his head, the royal "we" in his mouth, or the "strut" (lingering down to the eight-

eenth century to be admired by Sir Roger de Coverley) with which his royal legs must tread the stage. There is in all Elizabethan dramatic art something naïve — something self-descriptive — in the lines, which in the three centuries of evolution towards the more purely and strictly dramatic has nearly disappeared. The wicked, like Richard III in his first soliloquy, know that they are wicked; the good, that they are good; heroes like Julius Caesar boast and vaunt their prowess; and a king, like a god on the stage, must every minute remember, and make us remember too, that he is nothing less. Henry's preaching, swaggering, and swinging of the scepter may repel us a bit today; but that is because as we read we democratically take him for no more than a man, as people at the Globe did not nor were expected to do. Even we, at the theater, are perhaps not so different and enlightened as we think. King Edward VII, not emulating the ceremoniousness of his ancestors, walked and talked like other people; but on the stage, not more than a score of years ago, Richard Mansfield, as Henry V, found it expedient to strut and swagger a bit again, in the fashion that pleased Sir Roger.

Elmer Edgar Stoll, *"Henry V," Poets and Playwrights*, 1930.

. . . I see no running imagery in the first or second part of *Henry IV*. In *Henry V*, however, the opening words of the chorus — sighing for 'a Muse of fire' to 'ascend the brightest heaven of invention' — seem to give the key-note to the dominating atmosphere of the earlier and best part of the play, swift and soaring movement; and it is not mere chance, I think, that we find, through the play, an unusual number of images of the flight of birds, which for our forefathers symbolised the swiftest movement known to man.

The desire adequately to convey to the audience this particular combination of intense swiftness and dignity, with the consciousness of the limitations of the rude and primitive theatre, dominates the opening prologue. Indeed, the urgent appeal to the onlookers to use their imaginations and piece out with their thoughts the imperfections of actors and stage, is the main theme of the vivid and stirring poetry of all five prologues.

The brilliant description of the fleet on its way from Southampton to Harfleur opens,

Thus with imagined wing our swift scene flies
In motion of no less celerity
Than that of thought.

Later when, on the return journey, the king is crossing from Calais to Dover, the audience are urged to use their thoughts with the strength or swiftness of a bird's flight, to

Heave him away upon your winged thoughts
Athwart the sea.

Henry himself, when making ready for France, with all the expedition possible, falls into the same simile:

Let our proportions for these wars
Be soon collected, and all things thought upon
That may with reasonable swiftness add
More feathers to our wings.

He measures emotion — its height and depth — by the same picture of the flight of a bird; though the king's affections, he tells his soldiers, are 'higher mounted' than those of common folk, 'yet, when they stoop, they stoop with the like wing'; and when arguing later with them as to the king's responsibility for the fate of individuals in battle, he points out that those of his soldiers who have previously been evildoers — thieves or murderers — meet their deserts in war, though they may have 'defeated the law and outrun native punishment, though they can outstrip men, they have no wings to fly from God: war is His beadle, war is His vengeance'.

Finally, the Duke of York's moving cry, when he finds his friend dead on the battle field, sums up, in the last two words, with Shakespeare's characteristic magic, the whole force of this favourite image:

Tarry, dear cousin Suffolk!
My soul shall thine keep company to heaven;
Tarry, sweet soul, for mine, then fly abreast.

We may note, that, though birds are not mentioned in any one of these images, yet the picture of their sure and soaring flight, swift and strong, is in each intense and vivid.

The little scene of the Dauphin with his spirited horse (Act III, Scene 7) adds to this feeling of strong and soaring motion, and coming where it does, just before the description of the 'poor condemned English', sitting by their camp-fires, patient and sad, lean and pale as ghosts, it points the contrast vividly between them and the 'over-lusty' French. The Dauphin's horse bounds from the earth like a tennis ball ('as if his entrails were hairs'), he is 'le cheval volant, the Pegasus', 'he trots the air', 'the earth sings when he touches it', 'he is pure air and fire', and 'when I bestride him', declares his master proudly, 'I soar, I am a hawk'. And the next minute we are with 'Harry in the night', 'walking from watch to watch, from tent to tent', cheering his war-worn soldiers.

Caroline Spurgeon, "Flight Images in *Henry V,*" *Shakespeare's Imagery and What It Tells Us*, 1935.

With *Henry V*, therefore, Shakespeare reached the climax of exterior life; it is at once a conclusion and a beginning. It is not primarily a patriotic play, for the First Chorus knows nothing of patriotism nor of England, but only of a *Muse of fire which would ascend the brightest heaven of invention* by discovering a challenge between mighty monarchies. Patriotism certainly keeps breaking in, but rather like the army itself: the mass behind Henry is dramatically an English mass, and as the play proceeds he becomes more and more an English king. So much must be allowed to the patriots; it is, however, for them to allow that he becomes something else and more as well, and it is in that something more that his peculiar strength lies.

Before defining that, however, and his own words define it, it may be well to remark a few of the differences between *Henry V* and its precedent *Henry IV*. The newer manner of the blank verse itself is accentuated; it gains in speed. Less even than in *Henry IV* are there any involutions or adornments; its movements, like the action of the persons, admit of no delay. It has lost superfluity, though it has not yet gained analysis. No word blurs, but each word does not yet illuminate, as each was to illuminate in that later play of action and vision, *Antony and Cleopatra*. Here it is equivalent to the King's desire and the King's deed, and equals the one with the other. But there is, at first, no variation between the King and other characters, as there is variation between the Prince and Hotspur and Falstaff

in *Henry IV:* what the King is, he is, and the others are apart from him. In fact, the next differences between the two plays are (i) the omission of Hotspur, and (ii) the omission of Falstaff. It will be said that Hotspur is dead before *Henry IV* ends and Falstaff dies soon after *Henry V* begins. But whatever historical necessity or moral convenience compelled those two deaths, the result is to leave the stage free not only for King Henry himself, but for something else — for the development of the idea of honour. In *Henry IV* honour had been peculiarly the property of Hotspur, and it had seemed like being his property in a narrower sense. He had regarded it almost as if it were something he owned as he owned his armour, something that he could capture and possess.

> By heaven methinks it were an easy leap
> To pluck bright honour from the pale-fac'd moon,
> Or dive into the bottom of the deep,
> Where fathom-line could never touch the ground,
> And pluck up drowned honour by the locks;
> So he that doth redeem her thence might wear
> Without corrival all her dignities:

Against this splendid and egotistical figure is the figure of Falstaff. Up to the last act of *Henry IV*, Part II, the distinction of Falstaff had been that, though he may want a lot for this comfort, he does not need it for his complacency. Hotspur, without a sense of his own honour, feels himself deficient; it is why he rebels. Falstaff, without the same sense, feels himself free; it is how he runs away or fights as circumstances and his own common sense dictate. Henry V might have been made like either of them; in fact, he was made like neither. Neither Hotspur nor Falstaff could suit the muse of fire or the brightest heaven. Honour must for Henry in his own play be something consonant with that brightness, and that invention discovered a phrase which made honour more than reputation — whether for possession or repudiation.

> And those that leave their valiant bones in France,
> Dying like men, though buried in your dunghills,
> They shall be fam'd; for there the sun shall greet them,
> And draw their honours reeking up to heaven,
> Leaving their earthly parts to choke your clime.

Their bodies are dead; their honours live, but not as fame upon earth. The heaven of invention is to suggest this other heaven; the honour of poetry is to show the honour of the spirit in challenge. It is a little reminiscent of *Lycidas;* where also Fame is transmuted into something pleasing to "all-judging Jove." The honours which so live are the spirits and souls of the righteous — anyhow, of the righteous at Agincourt. It is to Henry that the identification is given; it is for him that honour is now a name for man's immortal part. If that venture of war which is the result of the challenge between two great worldly powers, two mighty monarchies, is defeated, this end at least is left to those who carry themselves well in that venture.

Charles Williams, *"Henry V," Shakespeare Criticism: 1919-1935*, ed. A. Bradbey, 1936.

. . . "Henry V" has its splendors and its secondary attractions, but the forces in it are not unified. The reason probably is that for Shakespeare they had ceased to be genuine forces. He marshals for his task a host of substitute powers, but the effect is often hollow. The style strains itself to bursting, the hero is stretched until he struts on tiptoe and is still strutting at the last insignificant exit, and war is emptied of its tragic content. The form of the historical drama had been the tragic form; its dress is borrowed here, but only borrowed. The heroic idea splinters into a thousand starry fragments, fine as fragments but lighted from no single source.

Everywhere efforts are made to be striking, and they succeed. But the success is local. "Henry V" does not succeed as a whole because its author lacks adequate dramatic matter; or because, veering so suddenly away from tragedy, he is unable to free himself from the accidents of its form; or because, with "Julius Caesar" and "Hamlet" on his horizon, he finds himself less interested than before in heroes who are men of action and yet is not at the moment provided with a dramatic language for saying so. Whatever the cause, we discover that we are being entertained from the top of his mind. There is much there to glitter and please us, but what pleases us has less body than what once did so and soon will do so with still greater abundance again.

The prologues are the first sign of Shakespeare's imperfect dramatic faith. Their verse is wonderful but it has to be, for it is

doing the work which the play ought to be doing, it is a substitute for scene and action. "O for a Muse of fire," the poet's apology begins. The prologues are everywhere apologetic; they are saying that no stage, this one or any other, is big enough or wealthy enough to present the "huge and proper life" of Henry's wars; this cockpit cannot hold the vasty fields of France, there will be no veritable horses in any scene, the ship-boys on the masts and the camp-fires at Agincourt will simply have to be imagined. Which it is the business of the play to make them be, as Shakespeare has known and will know again. The author of "Romeo and Juliet" had not been sorry because his stage was a piece of London rather than the whole of Verona, and the storm in "King Lear" will begin without benefit of description.

Mark Van Doren, "Henry V," Shakespeare, 1939.

The Arden editor of Shakespeare's *Life of King Henry the Fifth*, H. A. Evans, sums up the common view of the play when he says that "its interest is epic rather than dramatic; it is the nearest approach on the part of the author to a national epic." The historical mirrors that Shakespeare held up to England before he wrote of Henry V were mirrors in which the Elizabethans could see their own national problems being acted out on the stage before them, and in which they could witness the eternal justice of God in the affairs of the body politic. They showed the conflicts of the age which endangered the state, threatening its peace and security. But in *Henry V* the English are mirrored triumphant in a righteous cause, achieving victory through the blessing of God. A mood of exultation pervades the play. Henry V stands as the ideal hero in contrast with the troubled John, the deposed Richard, the rebel Henry IV; for the traditional conception of Henry V was of a hero-king, and about his dominant figure Shakespeare chose to fashion a hero-play. The theme of the play is war, and the progress of the warrior-hero is the progress of the play. Thus the play becomes in form and content epic.

Lily B. Campbell, "The Victorious Acts of King Henry V," Shakespeare's 'Histories':
Mirrors of Elizabethan Policy, 1947.

In his portrait of Henry V as general, Shakespeare demonstrated that whatever deficiencies the play might have in

representing army life were not due to lack of pains. In no other military portrait — Falstaff not excepted — can we say with more assurance that here the dramatist made a careful study of military theory, and sketched character with the theory constantly in mind. Not even Holinshed was more closely studied for this purpose. In fact, although from Holinshed (and partially from *The Famous Victories of Henry the Fifth*) came the outline of Henry V as a religious, efficient warrior, Shakespeare derived most of Henry's conduct and speech as a general from the precepts of military books.

The indebtedness which resulted was different not merely in degree from that of his other military portraits; it was different in kind. For the first time, Shakespeare risked the consequences of drawing a handbook-perfect officer. In all of his other portraits he selected types or ranks interesting for wayward traits, either of contentiousness or of fraudulent practices. To attempt making his main dramatic figure not only "the mirror of all Christian kings" (Act V, Prologue, 6) but the mirror of a Christian general, and to deprive him further of the dissensions available in a divided command, was to forfeit in advance most of the playwright's dependable stratagems for good drama. We shall, to be sure, find that Shakespeare discovered opportunities for a few instances of minor tension within this model portrait, but these are insufficient to make Henry one of Shakespeare's most interesting military studies.

Paul Jorgenson, "Military Rank," *Shakespeare's Military World*, 1956.

Review Questions and Answers

Question 1.
What is the purpose of the description of Falstaff's death in Act II, Scene 3?

Answer
Shakespeare had promised, at the close of *Henry IV*, Part II, to give his audience further scenes with Falstaff, who was a most popular character. In *Henry V*, however, the old, roguish knight would have been out of place. He would not fit the exalted mood of patriotism and honor and he could hardly be set in contact with the new king who, in this play, shows no sign of acquaintance with his old companions, Pistol and Bardolph. At the same time, the audience would hardly have been satisfied with having Falstaff treated like his lesser followers, to be hanged like Bardolph, or sent off to a life of beggary and stealing like Pistol. Because of the promise and audience expectancy, he also could not simply be ignored. It seems best to have him die before the war begins and to have that death reported in a manner that keeps in mind the rowdy quality of the old knight, while at the same time arousing pathos to hear of the friendly fellow's dying.

Question 2.
Why did Shakespeare introduce the French court ladies in Act III, Scene 4?

Answer
The only glimpse of women in the play for two and a half acts has been the sight of Pistol's wife, the hostess of the tavern. Shakespeare may have felt it was time to give the audience another feminine touch. Also, since the play deals mainly with nobles and great events, there should be a lady of rank brought in, with a movement toward peace set in contrast with the war-bound nobles. Katherine, furthermore, was to be married to Henry as part of the terms of the treaty of peace. He would have to meet her then and, dramatically, this would be rather a sudden introduction. We are therefore prepared for the later scene

between Henry and Katherine by this view of her here, trying to learn English in anticipation of her fate. Having these dramatic reasons for bringing Katherine in, Shakespeare makes use of the occasion to add his characteristic humor to the scene.

Question 3.

In the quarrel which develops between the disguised Henry and Williams, which one is in the right?

Answer

Williams and Henry quarrel over a remark made by Williams to the effect that a common soldier's opinion of the king will make little difference to his majesty. Henry had said that, if the king permits himself to be ransomed, "I will never trust his word after." As Williams thought Henry to be only a common soldier like himself, the remark naturally seemed ludicrous to him. Williams' objection was quite natural. But Henry, apparently forgetting for a moment that he was disguised and seemingly just another soldier, became annoyed and retorted: "Your reproof is something too round" — and the quarrel began. Henry's commanding nature popped out of his disguise. The right of the matter is with Williams.

Question 4.

What is the point of the whole episode concerning the exchange of gloves? (Act IV, Scene 8)

Answer

The quarrel that started with Williams and the exchange of gloves has led the audience to expect a sequel. Henry, however, cannot again put on a disguise just to meet the soldier, nor as king can he wear the glove and make himself vulnerable to a possible insult from a commoner. By having Henry give the glove to Fluellen, with word that its challenger will be a traitor, Shakespeare finds a good way out of the difficulty. In the first place, we are given another moment of humor. In the second, Henry is shown as a generous monarch since, instead of punishing Williams, he fills his glove with coins. Finally, the integrity and innate dignity of even the common soldier of England are made apparent in the manner in which Williams stands up to this treatment of him. When he sees Fluellen wear-

ing the glove, he immediately strikes him. He is firm in telling his story to the king and, when the king reveals that he was the offended "soldier," in insisting that any quarrel was with the "soldier," not the king: "I beseech you to take it for your own fault and not mine. For had you been as I took you for, I made no offence." He maintains his manliness to the end, accepting (we may assume) the king's gift as his due, under the circumstances, but bluntly refusing the twelve-penny tip Fluellen would thrust upon him. In this way, what at first seems like an almost irrelevant piece of poor jesting actually enforces the picture of the upright Englishman basic to the play.

Question 5.

Describe the Battle of Agincourt as it is portrayed in *Henry V*.

Answer

A vivid picture is presented of the opposing armies before the fight. The English, under the command of the king and the Duke of York, are represented as apparently a "poor and starved band," whose "lank-lean cheeks and war-worn coats," whose silence and "gesture sad" provide food for the mockery of their enemies. The French army, "over-confident and lusty," under the command of the Constable of France, is represented as a characteristic feudal force numbering "full three-score thousand," composed mainly of "princes, barons, lords, knights, squires, and gentlemen of blood and quality." Before the battle, the English king gently reproaches the Earl of Westmoreland for wishing for more help from England. The French herald, Montjoy, offers terms on behalf of the Constable of France. Henry replies with dignity, expressing his fixed determination not to surrender.

The engagement begins, York leading the English forces. The two armies are soon engaged in hand-to-hand conflict. The French are quickly thrown into confusion, their very numbers adding to their difficulties. Their horses plunging and struggling "fetlock deep in gore and with wild rage" add to the disorder and the slaughter. The rout is so complete that even the cowardly bully, Pistol, takes his noble prisoner and demands "egregious ransom." Many of the French nobility, among whom are Bourbon, the Constable of France and Orleans,

refuse to surrender and, with fiery, reckless courage, dash into the midst of the English army and offer up their lives "on heaps."

The battle is won, but the slaughter is not yet complete. French plunderers got into the rear to seize upon the baggage and killed the boys who were guarding the camp. Henry, believing that the enemy had been reinforced and were about to renew the attack, gives orders, which are promptly carried out, that every man should slay his prisoner. He is sending a message of defiance to the new enemy when the herald, Montjoy, comes humbly to ask for permission to bury the dead and to inform Henry that the victory is his. King Henry orders a general thanksgiving and ascribes his success to God alone.

Incidentally, we learn that Henry himself fought on foot like a common soldier and that he had a personal encounter with the Duke of Alençon, whom he slew. We are informed that 10,000 French were slain, including 26 princes and nobles, 8,400 knights, squires and gallant gentlemen, and but 1,600 mercenaries, while the loss of the English amounted to only a few, among whom were the Duke of York and the Earl of Suffolk.

Question 6.

Account for the success of the English army at the Battle of Agincourt.

Answer

The English were a unified group of men — a band of brothers. They were on friendly, even intimate terms with their officers, whom they trusted. They were a chosen force, hardened by serving together for some months and used to working as a team. The English archers were the best in Europe, superbly trained. Their general, the king, was a born tactician.

The French were a scratch force, unused to one another. The officers despised the common soldiers, whether they were nationals or mercenaries. The knights in armor, upon whom France chiefly relied, were deplorably lacking in discipline and training in concerted action. The French leaders were careless, lazy and indifferent to the lot of their men or even the circumstances under which they should fight. The French

gentlemen were all overconfident and, therefore, careless in their personal behavior.

The French command collected its forces in a confined space where there was insufficient room to manoeuvre and the cavalry were jammed together and rendered ineffective as well. They were a magnificent target for the English archers. There had been an overnight rain and the ground was deep in mud, soon churned up into a death trap for horses and men. The French forces were caught in this trap because of the incompetence of the French leadership in not using the one French advantage — their overwhelming numbers — to their benefit.

Question 7.
How does Shakespeare bring out the contrast between the English and French characters?

Answer
The character of the dauphin as representative of the French nation forms the strongest possible contrast to that of the English king who typifies all that is best in the English character. In the first act, the gift of tennis balls is evidence of the vain and haughty spirit of the dauphin, as well as of his utterly false conception of King Henry, whose prudence and forethought had just been demonstrated in his wise suggestions with regard to Scotland. The contrast is forcibly shown, too, in the defiant insolence of the dauphins' message: "For our losses, his exchequer is too poor; for the effusion of our blood, the muster of his kingdom too faint a number; and for our disgrace, his own person kneeling at our feet, but a weak and worthless satisfaction." This remark is contrasted with the self-depreciation combined with calm determination in the king's reply (Act III, Scene 6). On the one side we witness frivolity and vain boasts; on the other, pious humility and trust in divine aid. There is also a strong contrast between the French nobility — the Constable of France, Bourbon, Orleans and the rest — and the English lords of the stamp of Salisbury, Bedford, Exeter and Westmoreland. On the eve of Agincourt, we see the "confident and over-lusty French, proud of their numbers and secure in soul," casting dice for the prisoners they have not yet captured, while "the poor condemned English, like sacrifices, by their

watchful fires, sit patiently and inly ruminate the morning's danger.'' The idle chatter, proud boasting and aristocratic insolence of the French is a contrast to the unassuming use the English make of their native tongue, and would arouse at once in the audience a feeling that "here come the French, the baffled French braggarts.''

Question 8.
How are the common soldiers characterized in this play?

Answer
Shakespeare does not in this play give us complete individual portraits of any of the minor characters, but from the actions and words of Williams, Bates and the others, we are able to form a very good idea of the typical English soldier as conceived by the poet. There are two classes of soldiers exhibited in the play. Williams and Bates may be taken as representative of the courageous many, while Pistol, Nym and Bardolph represent the cowardly few. The better sort are brave and determined as mastiffs, blunt and plain-spoken but loyal and trustworthy, not overburdened with intellectual armor. They eat like wolves and fight like devils. They quarrel with one another and quickly return an injury, but readily become reconciled and shake hands again.

G.C. Moore remarks:

They are no mere foils to the hero, mere caricatures of humanity. Within their limits they use their minds, criticise their superiors, sometimes make points against them, see a truth when it is well put to them; know their duty, and are ready to do it even at the cost of a life which they also find sweet. They too are men.

The class of cowardly bullies of which Nym, Bardolph and Pistol are types is too accurately depicted by Gower (Act III, Scene 6, 64-77) to require further description.

Question 9.
What is the purpose of introducing a) Bardolph, Nym and the underworld characters; b) the chorus?

Answer

(a) In introducing the comic characters, Bardolph, Nym, Pistol and the hostess, Shakespeare was probably influenced by the following motives:

(1) To offer variety and comic relief to the serious and lofty topics which fill the greater part of the play.

(2) To deepen the sense of reality in the minds of the audience by presenting the trivial and commonplace next to the heroic and ideal, cowardice in company with courage. "Shakespeare wandered in pursuit of universal nature. The glancings of his eye are from earth to heaven, from heaven to earth," remarks Warton.

(3) In the Epilogue to *Henry IV*, Shakespeare promised that he would continue the story "with Sir John in it." But Falstaff had been, from the point of view of comedy, too important to be included again in a dramatic history of such lofty tone as that of *Henry V*. The poet, therefore, changed his mind and was content to introduce, in partial fulfilment of his promise, the minor characters referred to, most of whom had already figured as companions or servants of the fat knight.

(b) The chorus is introduced because the poet was unable, merely through the representation of the characters upon the stage to convey fully all the grandeur of character and all the magnificence of action which he wanted to portray. Hence, he was obliged to resort to the device of prologues spoken by the chorus, whereby he was enabled to add description to representation. The particular purposes answered by these prologues are —

(1) To explain the action of the play and "jumpin o'er times," to narrate events which are supposed to have taken place between the acts.

(2) To describe in word pictures voyages, battles and sieges, which cannot be represented on the stage.

(3) To apologize for imperfections of all kinds.

(4) To heighten, by a sort of personal description, the character of the king.